JAM JAM JAM

with
THIN LIZZY

Exclusive Distributors:
Music Sales Limited
8/9 Frith Street
London W1V 5TZ England

Music Sales Pty Limited
120 Rothschild Avenue
Rosebery, NSW 2018
Australia

Order No AM 949509 Jam with Thin Lizzy ISBN 0-7119-7470-5
This book © Copyright 1999 by Wise Publications
Visit the Internet Music Shop at
http://www.musicsales.co.uk

Cover Design by Kim Waller
Music engraved by Cambridge Notation

Printed in Malta by Interprint Limited

Your Guarantee of Quality
As publishers we strive to produce every book to the highest commercial standards. The music has been
freshly engraved and the book has been carefully designed to minimise awkward page turns and to make
playing from it a real pleasure. Particular care has been given to specifying acid-free, neutral-sized paper
made from pulps which have not been elemental chlorine bleached. This pulp is from farmed sustainable
forests and was produced with special regard for the environment.
Throughout, the printing and binding have been planned to ensure a sturdy, attractive publication which
should give years of enjoyment. If your copy fails to meet our high standards, please inform us and we will
gladly replace it.

Music Sales' complete catalogue describes thousands of titles and is available in full colour sections by
subject, direct from Music Sales Limited. Please state your areas of interest and send a cheque/postal
order for £1.50 for postage to: Music Sales Limited, Newmarket Road, Bury St Edmunds, Suffolk IP33 3YD.

Wise Publications
London/New York/Sydney/Paris/Copenhagen/Madrid

CONTENTS

ON THE CD

The CD is split into two sections; section 1 (tracks 1-8) is the backing tracks minus lead guitar & vocals, while section 2 (tracks 9-16) is the backing tracks with all guitar parts added, so in addition to the written tab you can hear the rhythm, fills and solos as they should be played!! After section 2 there is a bonus track, Brian Robertson plays a solo excerpt from Still In Love With You (track 17).

Music arranged and produced by Stuart Bull and Steve Finch.
Recorded at the TOTAL ACCURACY SOUNDHOUSE, Romford, England.

Mick Ash: bass.
Adam Bushell: drums.
Don't Believe A Word - Stuart Bull: guitar, Brian Robertson: guitar solo.
Waiting For An Alibi - Stuart Bull: guitar.
Still In Love With You - Jamie Humphries: all guitars and Solo No.2, Stuart Bull: Solo No.1.
The Boys Are Back In Town - Jamie Humphries: all guitars, Stuart Bull: guitar 2 Main Solo.
Whisky In The Jar - Eric Bell: guitar.
Jailbreak - Stuart Bull: guitar.
Rosalie - Jamie Humphries: guitar.
Emerald - Jamie Humphries: guitar.

Music transcribed by Jamie Humphries
Jamie Humphries plays Ernie Ball Musicman Guitars

Professional Guitar Workshops

Visit the Total Accuracy
Audio Visual Experience at
http://www.totalaccuracy.co.uk

Introduction

THE TOTAL ACCURACY 'JAM WITH...' series is a powerful learning tool that will help you extend your stockpile of licks and fills and develop your improvisational skills. The combination of musical notation and guitar tablature in the book, together with backing tracks on the CD, gives you the opportunity to learn each track note for note and then jam with a professional session band. The track listing reflects some of Thin Lizzy's most popular recordings, providing something for guitarists to have fun with and improvise with, as well as something to aspire to.

The first eight tracks on the CD are full length backing tracks recorded minus lead guitar. The remaining tracks feature the backing tracks with the lead guitar parts added. Although many of you will have all the original tracks in your own collections, we have provided them in the package for your reference. The 'JAM WITH...' series allows you to accurately recreate the original, or to use the transcriptions in this book in conjunction with the backing tracks as a basis for your own improvisation. For your benefit we have put definite endings on the backing tracks, rather than fading them out as is the case on some of the original recordings. The accompanying transcriptions correspond to our versions. Remember, experimenting with your own ideas is equally important for developing your own style; most important of all, however, is that you enjoy JAM with THIN LIZZY and HAVE FUN!

Thin Lizzy were formed by two school friends, Phil Lynott, vocals and bass, and Brian Downey, drums, in Dublin, Ireland in 1969. The two friends had previously played together in Skid Row, Sugar Shack and Orphanage. They teamed up with ex-Them guitarist Eric Bell, and were signed to Decca records in 1970. Their first two albums, *Thin Lizzy*, 1971, and *Shades Of A Blue Orphanage*, 1972, were not particularly well received. But in 1973 they had a massive UK Top 10 hit with a reworking of the traditional Irish tune *Whiskey In The Jar*. The song featured a catchy "nasal" guitar riff, along with Lynott's lazy vocal style. This success was duplicated with the release of their next album *Vagabonds Of The Western World*.

At the end of 1973 Eric Bell left, and was replaced by ex-Skid Row guitarist Gary Moore in the early part of 1974. Gary Moore was only with the band for four months, before he left to join the jazz/rock fusion band Colosseum. The band briefly featured two other guitarists, Andy Gee and John Cann, before settling for the now legendary dual guitar line up of Brian Robertson and Scott Gorham. The two new guitarists appeared with the band at the 1974 Reading Rock Festival, and on the band's first release for their new record label Vertigo, entitled *Night Life*.

In 1975 they released the *Fighting* album, which was their UK album chart debut. But the sales of *Fighting* were nothing compared to the success of their classic 1976 release *Jailbreak*. The album was a Top 20 hit in both the UK and the US, and included possibly their most famous single ever, *The Boys Are Back In Town*, which featured a memorable harmony guitar hook that made Robertson and Gorham one of the most renowned guitar duets in the rock business. This album also spawned two other hit singles, *Cowboy Song*, and the title track *Jailbreak*.

In 1976 the band released their next album, *Johnny The Fox*, but its success was overshadowed by Lynott's increasing drug use. The following year disaster struck, with Robertson severing tendons in his left hand following a fight, on the eve of a US tour supporting rock legends Queen. Gary Moore rejoined for a brief stint, but left to return to Colosseum, and Robertson was back in the ranks. In the same year Lizzy released *Bad Reputation*, which reached number four in the UK chart, their best position yet.

Lynott felt that a lot of the bands energy and rawness was lost on the studio recordings and so, in 1978 Lizzy released *Live and Dangerous*. The album was a collection of all the classic Lizzy tracks, performed with breathtaking accuracy, and Lynott's overwhelming stage presence. The album also included what would become the definitive version of the ballad *Still In Love With You*, which saw Robertson and Gorham perform spine-tingling solos with such feel and passion, that, to this day, they are still regarded as some of the best live rock recordings ever. In 1979 Robertson left, and was once again replaced by Gary Moore.

In 1979 Lizzy released *Black Rose*, which contained the single *Waiting For An Alibi*, a powerful rocker, with twisting lead harmony lines. Gary Moore was sacked mid-tour in the U.S., and Lynott's old friend Midge Ure was flown out to the States to complete the tour. It was rumoured that Midge learnt the set on the flight! After a couple of tours Midge left to pursue a solo career with the pop act Ultravox, and was replaced by live Pink Floyd guitarist Snowy White. White appeared on the 1980 release *Chinatown*, which included the controversial single *Killer On The Loose*.

In 1981 Thin LIzzy released *Renegade*, with new guitarist John Sykes, who later joined Whitesnake. 1983 saw the release of Lizzy's last album, *Thunder and Lightning*, and Lynott and Downey went on to form Grand Slam. In the latter part of his career, Lynott embarked on a few solo projects, one of which yielded the track *Yellow Pearl*, which became famous as the title track to Top Of The Pops. In 1985 Lynott settled his differences with Moore, and recorded the single *Out In The Fields*. Sadly on January 4 1986 Phil Lynott died, at the age of 34, after an eight day heroin-induced coma.

This book contains eight classic Lizzy tracks transcribed in full. The accompanying CD also includes two original members of Thin Lizzy, who came to the Total Accuracy Soundhouse to appear on two of the specially recorded backing tracks. Eric Bell re-recorded *Whiskey In The Jar*, and Brian Robertson re-recorded the solo *Don't Believe A Word*. The CD also includes a specially recorded version of the solo to *Still In Love With You*. This book marks another milestone in the Thin Lizzy legacy.

Performance Notes

Don't Believe A Word

This fast driving track features a pumping 12/8 time signature. The track kicks off with a powerful riff based around A dorian; (A, B, C, D, E, F♯, G, A). The latter half of the intro introduces a second guitar part, performing a harmony line using diatonic thirds.

The main verse riff features a variation on the intro, and uses notes from the A minor pentatonic scale; (A, C, D, E, G, A). A rhythm guitar performs the ringing chords of Am7, Dm7, and G major underneath. The verse also features a short harmony line, using notes from D dorian; (D, E, F, G, A, B, C, D). The harmony is based on diatonic thirds, with guitars two and three playing the same line an octave apart, This section is followed by the descending chords of A5, G5, F5, D minor and C5.

After the second verse, another section based around the E minor pentatonic scale; (E, G, A, B, D, E) is introduced. The riff is doubled an octave higher by a second guitar. Another riff is introduced at bar 27, based around the D minor pentatonic scale; (D, F, G, A, C, D) and is also doubled by a second harmony guitar.

The solo starts at bar 32, and demonstrates Brian Robertson's excellent use of the wah pedal. The solo uses mainly A dorian, and the A minor pentatonic scale, and kicks off with a fast tremolo picked bend that is gradually released. The solo utilises fast legato phrasing, with blues-based bends.

At bar 41, Brian includes the F natural note, which could be seen as originating from the A aeolian mode; (A, B, C, D, E, F, G, A). The solo concludes with a repicked bend, performed with vigorous vibrato.

After the final verse, the song finishes with an outro using the chords of A5, G5 and F5, before resolving with a riff similar to the one found in the intro. This track was recorded using Gibson Les Pauls and Marshall amps.

Waiting For An Alibi

This track was taken from the *Black Rose* album, and features some powerful rock rhythm and lead playing. The track starts with a signature Lizzy twin guitar melody, based around the C♯ aeolian mode; (C♯, D♯, E, F♯, A, B, C♯), with both guitars performing a harmony line diatonic thirds apart.

The verse riff features the chords of C♯5, E5, G♯minor, G♯5 and B5, performed with a tight staccato feel, with rhythmical mutes played between them. The second half of the verse has a more loose, open feel, and also includes the chords of F♯5, A major and B major. An important thing to notice about this section is that the chords often change on the last eighth note of the bar, creating a push.

The chorus is based around the chords of E5, G♯5, A5 and B5, with E5 and G♯5 being performed with a tight palm muted eighth note rhythm. The chorus then leads back to the harmony melody found in the intro. The second verse has a similar progression to the first verse, but includes a short lick using notes from the C♯ minor pentatonic scale; (C♯, E, F♯, G♯, B, C♯).

The guitar solo starts at bar 69, after the second chorus, and includes fast blues/rock inspired licks, using notes from C♯ minor pentatonic, and C♯ aeolian. The main bulk of the solo uses fast legato lines, fused with string bending ideas. At bar 77 a fast descending pentatonic idea is introduced, and is harmonised by a second guitar at bar 80, using third and fourth intervals.

During the last chorus a short lead fill is included at bar 85-88, using notes from the E major pentatonic scale; (E, F♯, G♯, B, C♯, E). There is also another lead fill using the E major pentatonic scale, at bar 93, which is doubled an octave higher by guitar two. This lick is repeated at bar 97.

At bar 100 the outro melody line is introduced, with the two guitars playing a harmony part based around the E major scale; (E, F♯, G♯, A, B, C♯, D♯, E). This melody ascends the scale, with a third guitar harmony being introduced at bar 112. The song concludes with an idea based on the intro melody at bar 116. This song was probably recorded with Gibson Les Pauls, and Marshall amps.

Still In Love With You

The version transcribed in this book was taken from the *Live and Dangerous* album, and features some classic solo moments. The song starts with a short intro solo, performed over ringing A minor and F major chords, with the second half of the melody being played an octave lower by the second guitar. This melody, and the solo after, use notes from the A aeolian mode; (A, B, C, D, E, F, G, A). The progression is based around the chords of A minor, Dm7, Dm7/G and Cmaj7. The main guitar follows this progression throughout, but embellishes it with additional chordal fills, and blues based licks. The scale choice here is based mainly around A aeolian, and the minor pentatonic scale; (A, C, D, E, G, A). This guitar also plays different voicings and inversions of the chords performed by guitar two. The end of each verse is signalled by a ringing Fmaj7 chord. The rest after this final chord varies from verse to verse, and on some occasions in the transcription, a different time signature has been shown.

The first solo enters at bar 46, and is one of Brian Robertson's finest moments. The solo is full of tasteful blues phrases, based around A aeolian, and A minor pentatonic. Brian demonstrates his skill in soulful string bending, plus some pretty fast higher register pentatonic lines. The end of the solo includes fast tremolo picking section at bar 67, resolved with more searing bends and blues-based ideas.

The second solo is performed by Scott Gorham, and starts at bar 94. Once again, this solo uses notes from A aeolian and the A minor pentatonic scale. The solo also has a strong blues feel, and features some interesting passages that outline the underlying chord progression. There are also some prebend ideas at bars 95 and 100 plus some fast legato passages, including the ascending trill section at bars 112-114. The rhythm guitar under the first half of the solo performs the chords of Am7, Dm7, Em7 and F major, with a loose funk-style rhythm. The second half of the solo is performed over the chords of Cmaj7 and Fmaj7. These chords are performed with a tight syncopated sixteenth note rhythm that has a slight reggae feel.

The solo section is concluded with a twin guitar polyrhythmic idea at bars 124-130. This leads to a short melody line played freely, with guitar one concluding with a phrase based around an Am7 arpeggio; (A, C, E, G). This track was recorded with both guitarists using Gibson Les Pauls and Marshall amps.

The Boys Are Back In Town

This is probably Lizzy's most famous track, and was a massive hit for the band. The song kicks off with the chords of A5, B5 and D5, and a melodic line based on the A major pentatonic scale; (A, B, C♯, E, F♯, A). A second guitar performs the same chords, allowing them to sustain. The chords change on the last eighth note of the bar creating a push (this technique is an important part of the Thin Lizzy sound). The tune should be performed with a swung eighth note rhythm.

The verse progression uses some interesting chord types, not normally associated with rock guitar. The main verse riff uses the chords of A5, C♯m7, D major, F♯m7, Bm7 and Bm7/E, or B11, as it is sometimes called. A second guitar doubles this part, and occasionally hits the F♯sus4 chord against the F♯m7 played by guitar one. The second half of the verse features a similar progression to the first half, but also includes the F major chord.

The chorus is based on a progression similar to the intro, but also includes the D/A chord, and is performed without the short melodic line. This section is followed by the now famous twin guitar harmony line, that uses notes from the A major scale; (A, B, C♯, D, E, F♯, G♯, A).

During the second verse, a short lead fill is played, using notes from the A major pentatonic scale. This verse is followed by another chorus and harmony lead section. The bridge is introduced, with Dsus4/A and D major chords performed with a fast triplet rhythm. The bridge uses the same chords found in the verse, but also includes a fast triplet idea based around the F♯ minor chord, picking out notes on the A and D strings. The second time this section is played, the F♯ minor chord builds to the final verse.

After the final verse there is a down section before the solo. This is based around the A5, A6, B5 and D5 chords, with some short fill ideas. The solo begins with a twin guitar harmony line, based on the A major scale. This leads to an idea based on the main harmony theme, found earlier in the song. For the purpose of the transcription, this has been arranged for two guitars, as it was when played live (the *Live and Dangerous* album was the basis for this example). The melody line played by each guitar, ascends up the A major scale by third and fourth intervals, diatonic to A major. The solo concludes with string bends and a short melodic line, played using a harmony diatonic thirds apart, before resolving to the final A5 chord. This track was probably recorded using Gibson Les Paul guitars and Marshall amps.

Whiskey In The Jar

This track was the first hit for Thin Lizzy, (based on a traditional Irish folk song) and was the result of the band messing around at a rehearsal. The song kicks off with an intro melody based around the A aeolian mode; (A, B, C, D, E, F, G, A), and G major; (G, A, B, C, D, E, F♯, G). This part was originally recorded by two guitars, doubling the melody. The part is played freely, against an acoustic guitar, performing the chords of A minor, G major and E minor. The stabbing chords of G and F major lead to the main theme.

The main melodic hook is based around E aeolian; (E, F♯, G, A, B, C, D, E), and G major, and uses a very nasal tone. This melody is repeated at various points throughout the song. The main rhythm guitar is based on a clever mandolin-style part, that plays a melody on the B string against an open G string. The main progression uses the chords of G major, E minor and C major. The chorus uses the chords of D and C major, with the main guitar performing a melody on the G string, against an open D string. This then shifts to an ascending melody on the G and B strings. After the chorus, the main guitar hook is re-introduced, with the rhythm guitar performing a part based around the open D and G strings.

The solo features a clever Celtic flavoured idea, using notes from E aeolian, and G major. The solo has a strong melodic line, using string bends, and some fast left hand legato phrases. The main guitar hook is performed after the solo, and is doubled by a harmony guitar.

For the outro, the rhythm guitar plays a figure on the open D and G strings, with some rhythmic variations. The lead guitar plays another strong hook, with some fast sixteenth note triplet phrases, pulling off the open G string.

This track was recorded by Eric Bell, using a Fender Strat, plugged into an HH amp, through Carlsbro and Sound City cabs. A Copicat echo unit, and a Coloursound Tone Vista were also used.

Jailbreak

This is the title track from the classic *Jailbreak* album. This track starts with a sustaining bend, over an E5 chord, using notes from the E minor pentatonic scale; (E, G, A, B, D, E). The song then launches into a tight and punchy riff using the chords of A5, E5 and F♯5 with rhythmical muted notes between the changes. A short lead fill enters at bar 8, using notes from the F♯ minor pentatonic scale; (F♯, A, B, C♯, E, F♯). This lick should be performed with a wah pedal.

The verse progression is based around the same riff. The chorus uses the ringing chords of B5 and E5, with guitar one playing a melody and licks around the F♯ minor pentatonic scale. At the end of the chorus, guitar two outlines the chords of A major, E/G♯ and F♯ minor with a short melodic run, including an A major arpeggio; (A, C♯, E), and notes from the A major scale; (A, B, C♯, D, E, F♯, G♯, A).

After another verse and chorus with more F♯ minor pentatonic lead phrases, an instrumental section is introduced. This section starts with the melodic line found at the end of the chorus, leading to a driving eighth note riff based around the E, and A major chords, using the respective root notes as pedal tones.

The song is concluded with another verse, and an extended chorus section. This track was probably recorded with the Les Paul, Marshall combination.

Rosalie

This up tempo rocker can be found on the *Live and Dangerous* album, and was originally recorded by its composer, Bob Seger. The song starts with a riff based around the chords of D/A, and A major, with a driving A root note. Guitar two plays a sustaining A5 chord, before doubling guitar one's riff an octave higher. For this transcription, the main guitar stave has been arranged for one guitar, taking the key elements of both parts.

The verse is based around a similar idea to the intro, using the D/A, and A major chords, plus the main riff played an octave higher. The second half of the verse features a riff based around the E5, E6 and D5 chords, with a short melodic run outlining the chords. The chorus is based around the higher register A/D, and the A major chords, with an open position A5 chord.

The bridge section is introduced at the end of bar 64, and uses the chords of A5, A6, E5 and E6, and leads to the main solo section. The solo starts at bar 74, and is performed with a heavy dose of wah-wah. The solo uses notes from the major scale; (A, B, C♯, D, E, F♯, G♯, A), and the A major pentatonic scale; (A, B, C♯, E, F♯, A), and includes soulful bends and phrasing, producing a memorable and melodic solo. The bend at bar 80 should be repicked, and let down gradually, with some aggressive vibrato.

After the final verse and chorus, the band launch into an ad-libbed audience participation section, with the two guitars performing a descending melodic harmony line, based around the A major scale. This section is also embellished with some chordal fills. The song concludes with another melodic harmony line, that leads to a fast position shifting A major pentatonic lick, resolving with a riff similar to the intro section. This song was performed with Gibson Les Paul guitars and Marshall amps.

Emerald

This track has a very Celtic feel about it, with its driving 12/8 rhythm. For the purpose of the transcription the main guitar riff has been arranged for one guitar, as it is doubled on the original recording. The verse and intro are based around the chords of C5, B5, A5 and G5, played against driving root notes of the chords. The verse has a slightly more powerful feel, with the chords being performed with rhythmic variations. After the E5 chord at the end of each verse, an Irish inspired twin guitar melody is introduced, using notes from the A minor pentatonic scale; (A, C, D, E, G, A).

After the second guitar melody section, a short instrumental break is introduced, with a pounding twin guitar riff based around the chords of A5, C5 and D5, with guitar one switching a phaser effect. This riff section concludes with a 9/8 bar, before resolving back to 12/8 for the final E minor chord.

The solo section starts with another Celtic inspired twin guitar melody, based around A aeolian; (A, B, C, D, E, F, G, A). The harmony lines are based on third and fourth intervals diatonic to the key of A minor. The parts use hammer-ons and pull-offs, fused with slides, to produce a smooth flowing part. This section leads into the final solo section, which sees both guitars trading classic blues/rock licks based around A minor pentatonic and A dorian; (A, B, C, D, E, F♯, G, A). At several points, (bars 86 and bars 88-89) chromatic passing notes are added during some of the longer runs, to help build tension. At bars 90-94, a unison bend idea is introduced, which should be lowered gradually, before resolving to more pull-off ideas, and searing bends on the top E string. Bars 105 and 110 introduce a tricky string bending idea, where the G string is bent a full tone by pulling it down with the first finger.

The song is concluded with the Celtic based twin guitar hook, found earlier in the song. This track was probably recorded using the classic Gibson Les Paul guitar, and Marshall stack set up.

Notation & Tablature Explained

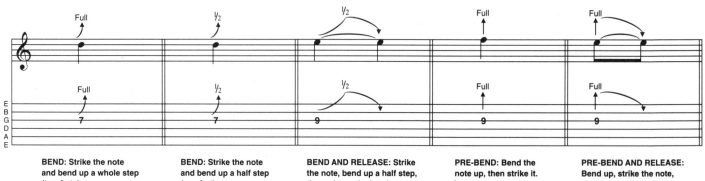

BEND: Strike the note and bend up a whole step (two frets).

BEND: Strike the note and bend up a half step (one fret).

BEND AND RELEASE: Strike the note, bend up a half step, then release the bend.

PRE-BEND: Bend the note up, then strike it.

PRE-BEND AND RELEASE: Bend up, strike the note, then release it.

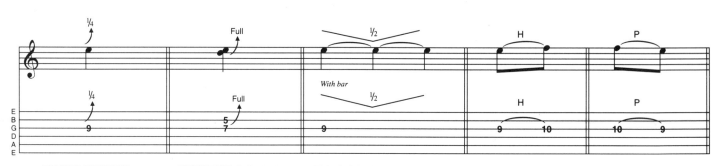

QUARTER-TONE BEND: Bend the note slightly sharp.

UNISON BEND: Strike both notes, then bend the lower note up to the pitch of the higher one.

TREMOLO BAR BENDS: Strike the note, and push the bar down and up by the amounts indicated.

HAMMER-ON: Strike the first note, then sound the second by fretting it without picking.

PULL-OFF: Strike the higher note, then pull the finger off while keeping the lower one fretted.

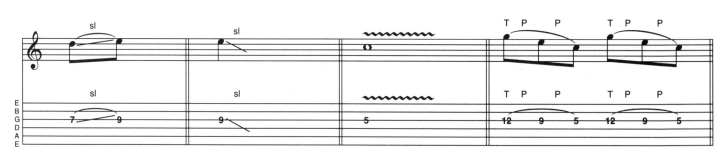

SLIDE: Slide the finger from the first note to the second. Only the first note is struck.

SLIDE: Slide to the fret from a few frets below or above.

VIBRATO: The string is vibrated by rapidly bending and releasing a note with the fretboard hand or tremolo bar.

TAPPING: Hammer on to the note marked with a T using the picking hand, then pull off to the next note, following the hammer-ons or pull-offs in the normal way.

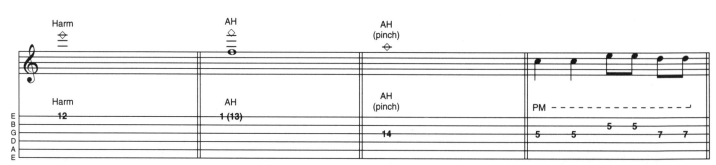

NATURAL HARMONIC: Lightly touch the string directly over the fret shown, then strike the note to create a "chiming" effect.

ARTIFICIAL HARMONIC: Fret the note, then use the picking hand finger to touch the string at the position shown in brackets and pluck with another finger.

ARTIFICIAL HARMONIC: The harmonic is produced by using the edge of the picking hand thumb to "pinch" the string whilst picking firmly with the plectrum.

PALM MUTES: Rest the palm of the picking hand on the strings near the bridge to produce a muted effect. Palm mutes can apply to a single note or a number of notes (shown with a dashed line).

Don't Believe A Word

Words and Music by PHIL LYNOTT

Don't be-lieve me if I

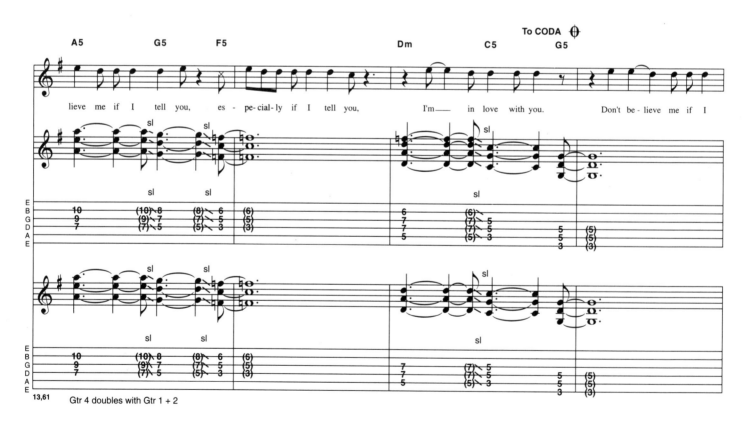

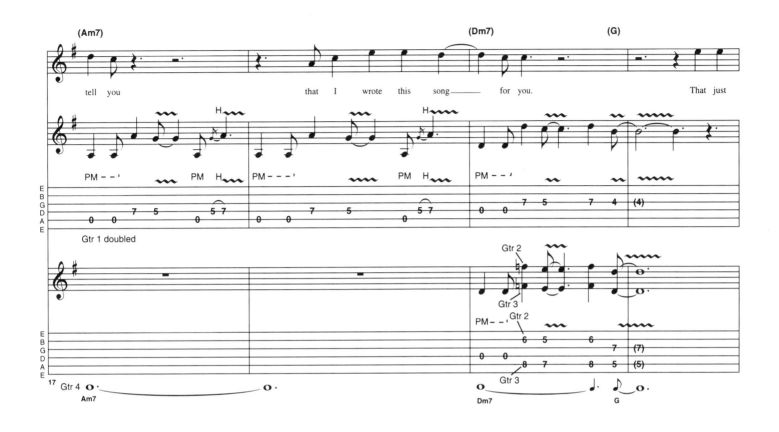

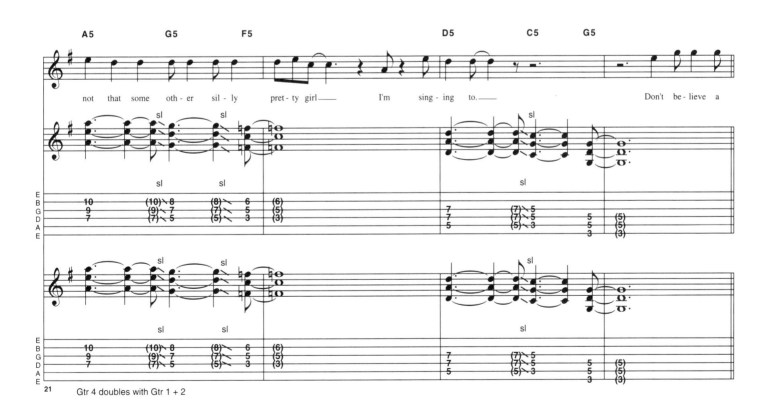

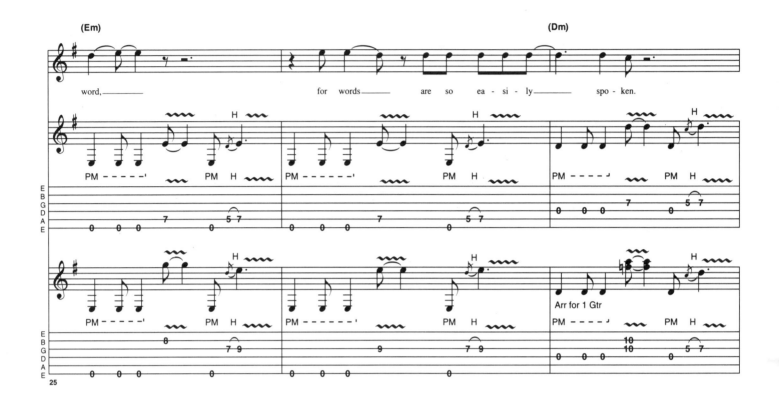

word,_____ for words_____ are so ea - si - ly_____ spo - ken.

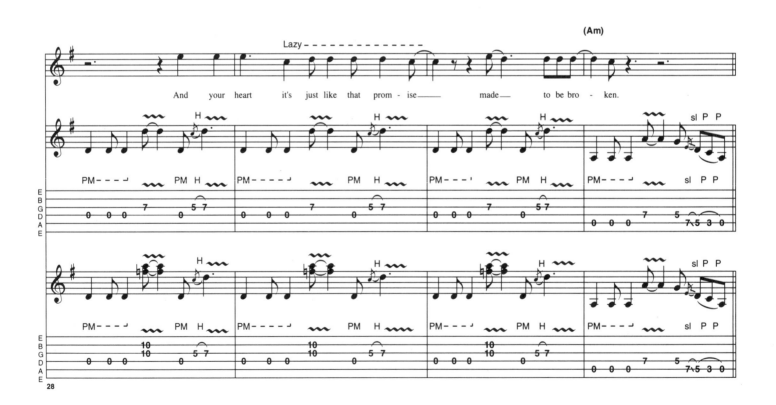

And your heart it's just like that prom - ise_____ made_____ to be bro - ken.

Gtrs 2 + 3 as previous verse

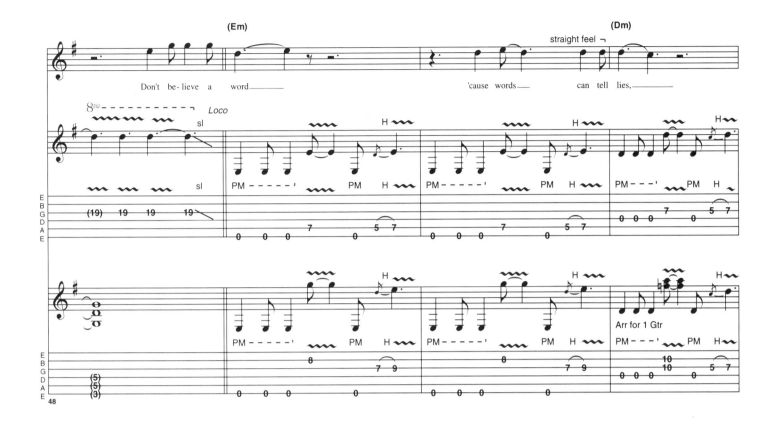

Don't be-lieve a word _____ 'cause words___ can tell lies,___

D 𝄋 al CODA

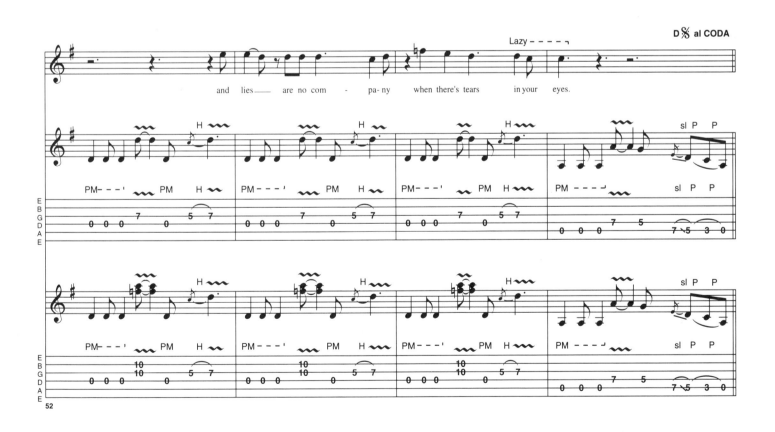

and lies___ are no com - pa-ny when there's tears in your eyes.

CODA

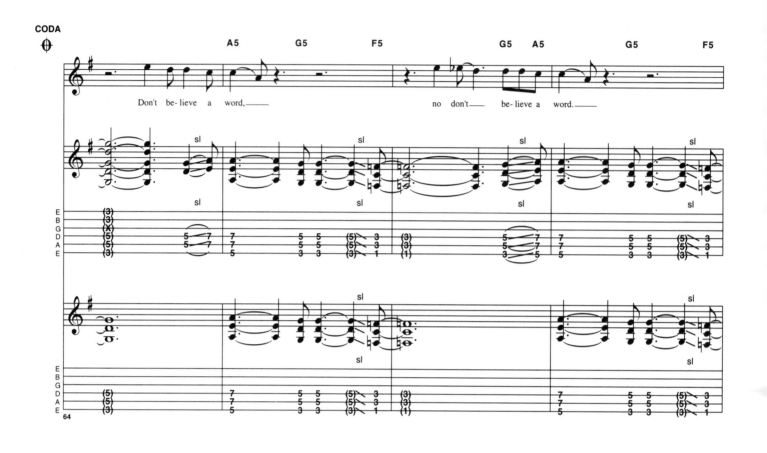

Don't be - lieve a word,____ no don't____ be - lieve a word.

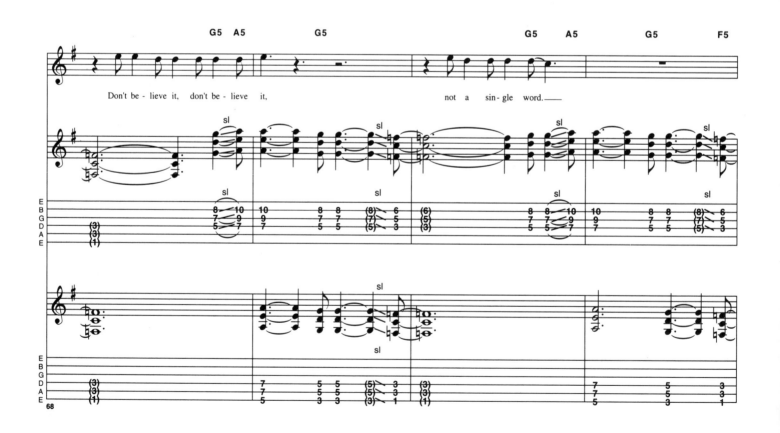

Don't be - lieve it, don't be - lieve it, not a sin - gle word.____

(Am)

Hey!   Don't   try.

Waiting For An Alibi

Words and Music by PHIL LYNOTT

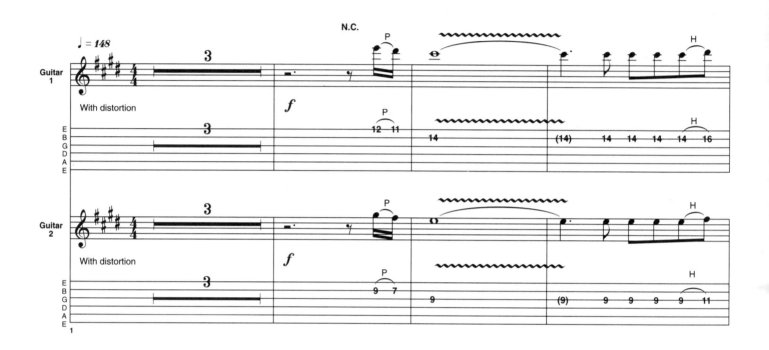

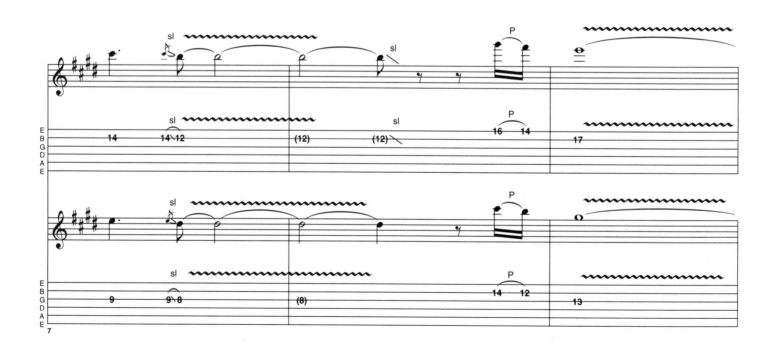

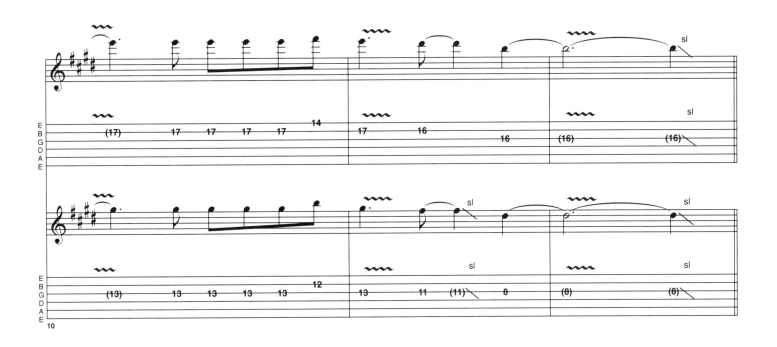

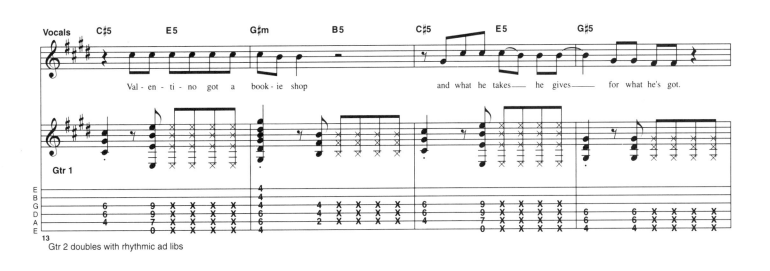

Gtr 2 doubles with rhythmic ad libs

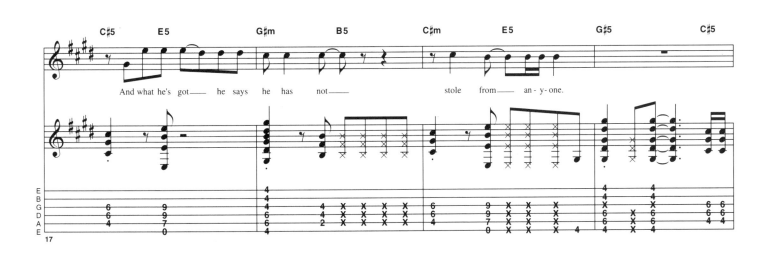

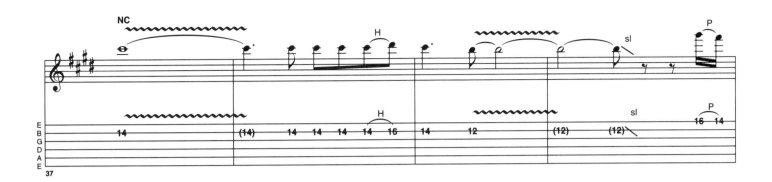

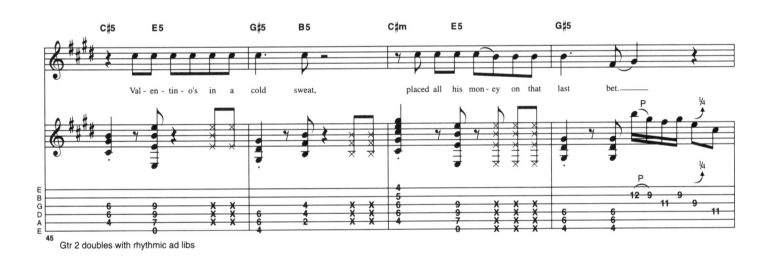

Gtr 2 doubles with rhythmic ad libs

Val - en - tin - o's in a cold sweat, placed all his mon - ey on that last bet.

'Gainst all the odds he smokes a - no - ther cig - ar - ette,— that's what helps him to for - get he's a ner - vous— wreck.

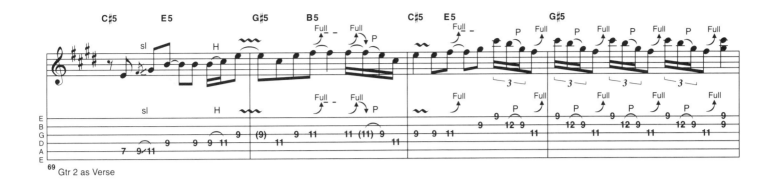

Gtr 2 as Verse

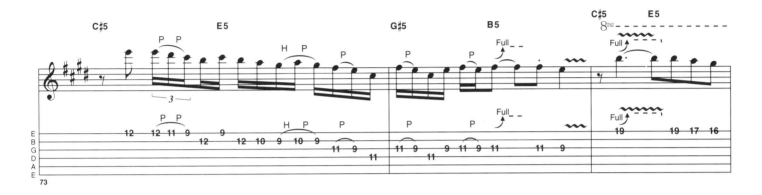

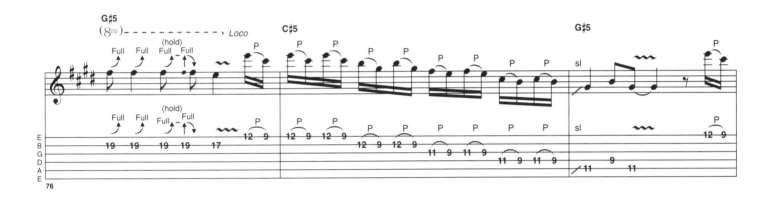

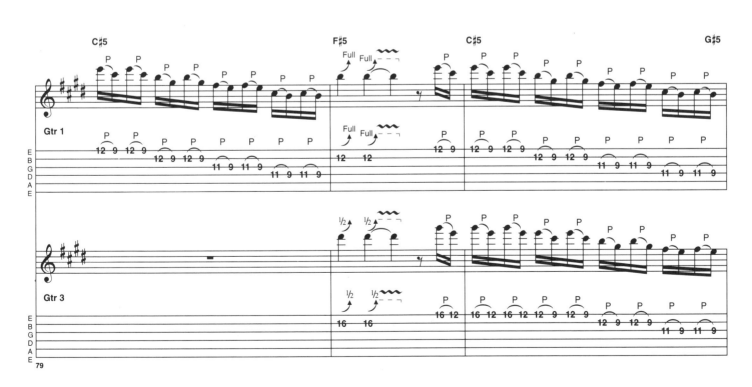

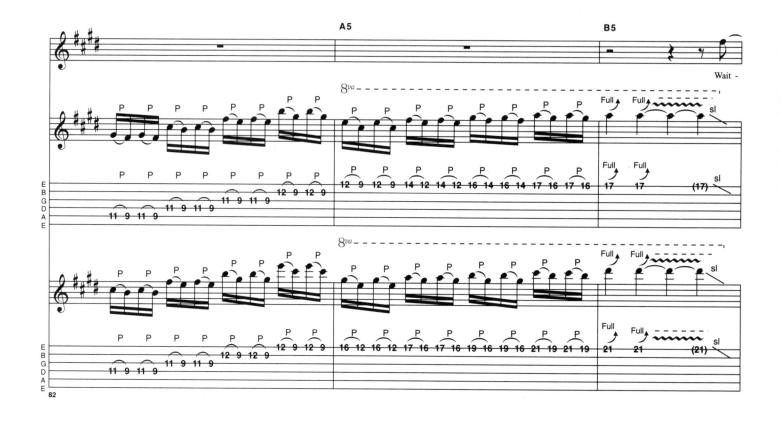

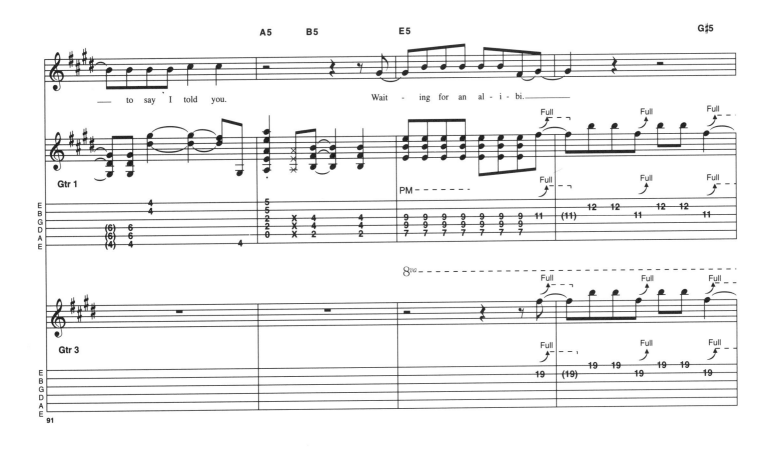

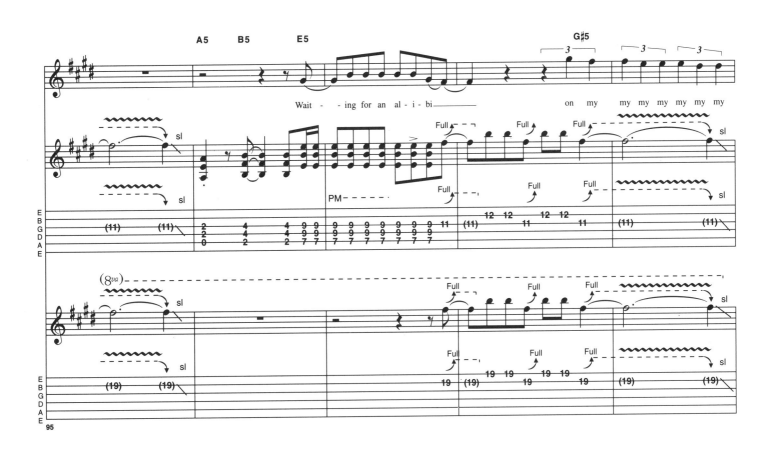

27

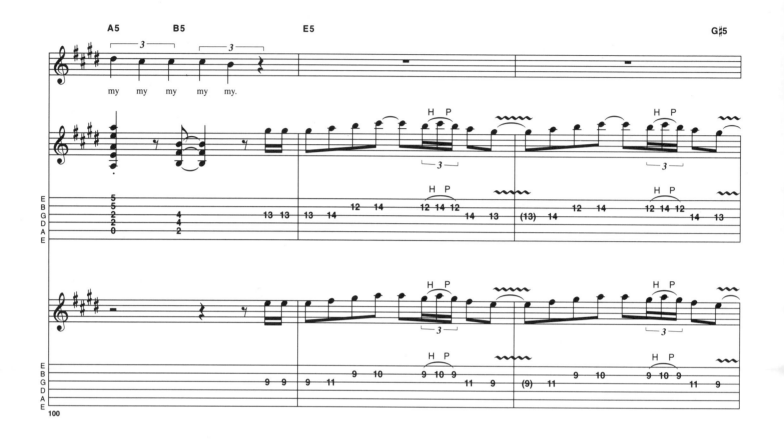

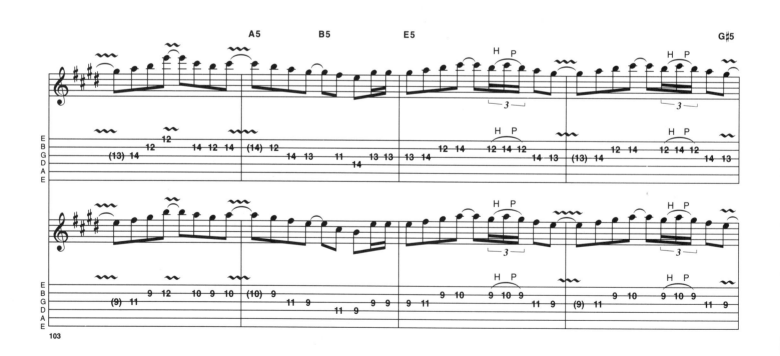

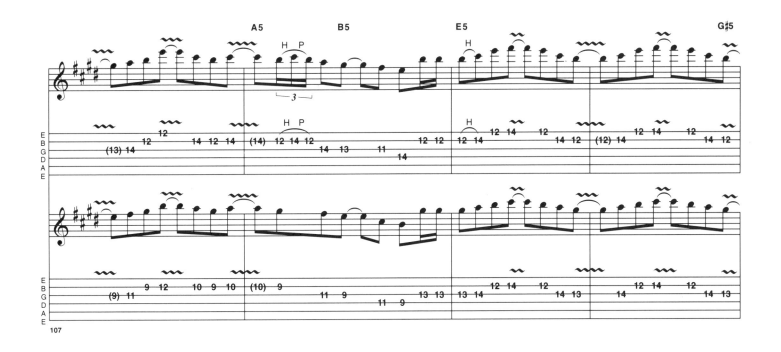

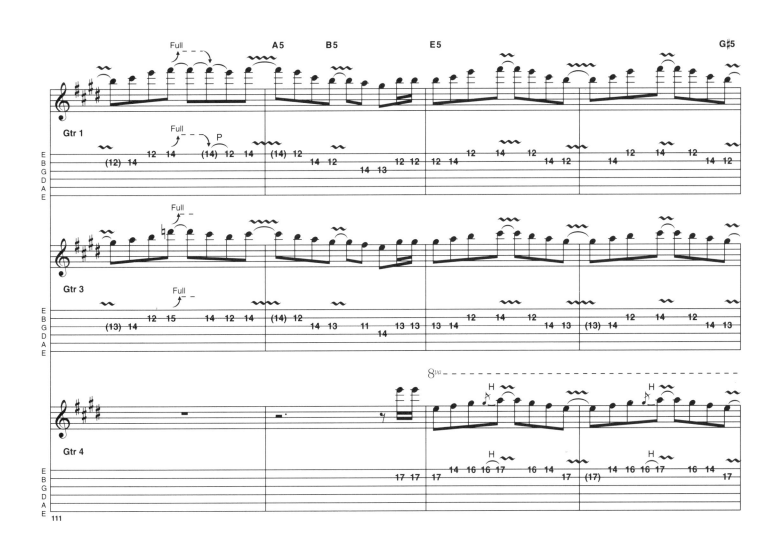

Still In Love With You

Words and Music by PHIL LYNOTT

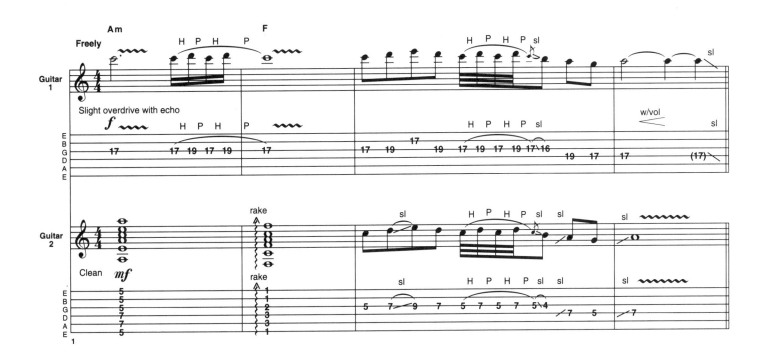

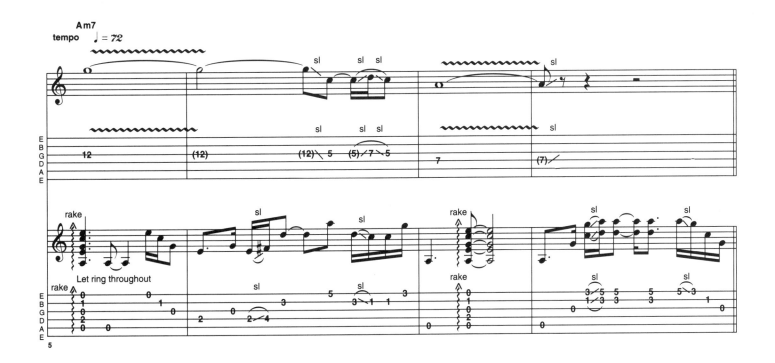

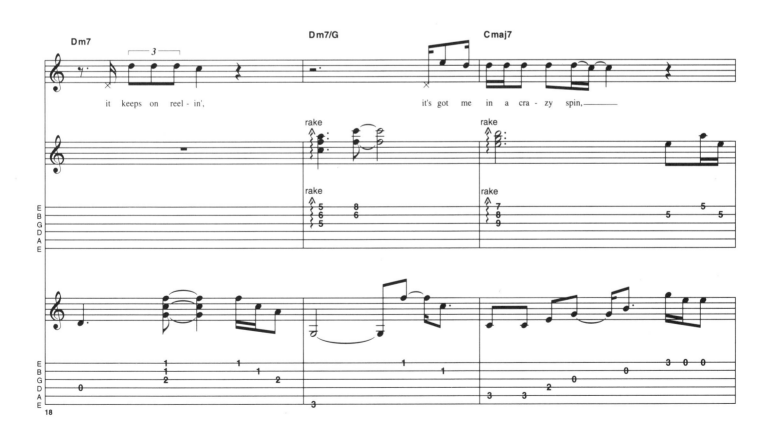

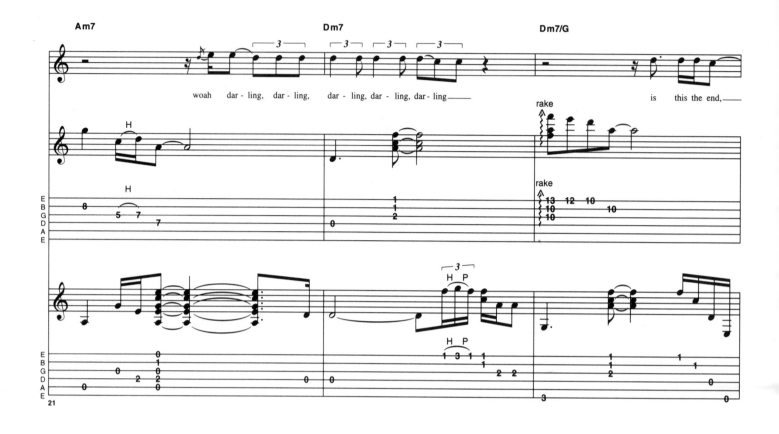

woah dar - ling, dar - ling, dar - ling, dar - ling, dar - ling——— is this the end,———

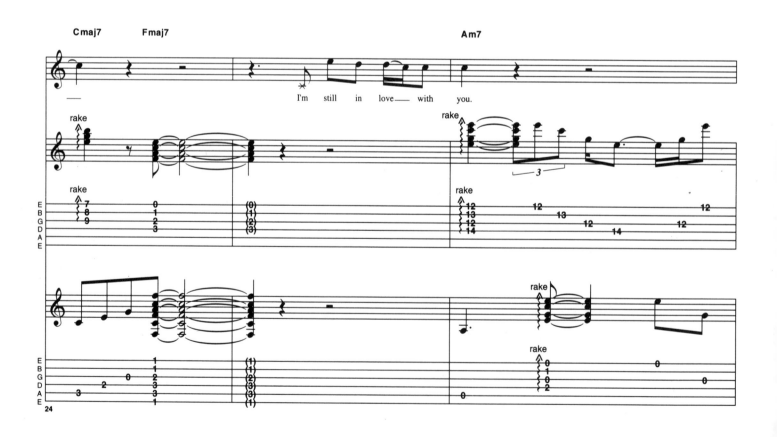

— I'm still in love—— with you.

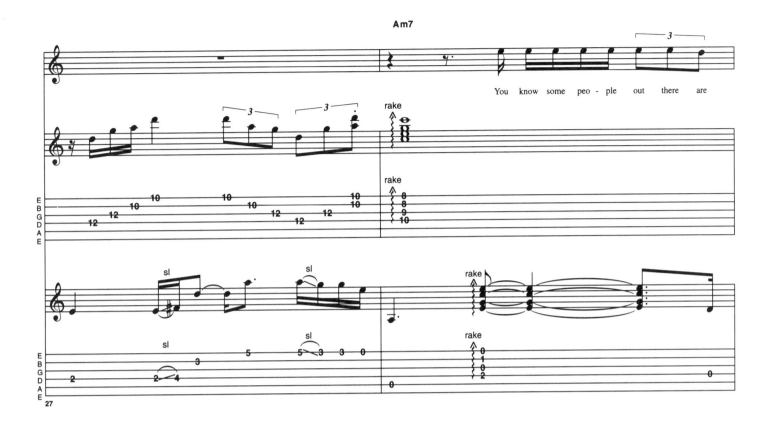

You know some peo - ple out there are

say - ing   time has it's way of heal - ing,   it can dry— all the   tears   from your eyes.—

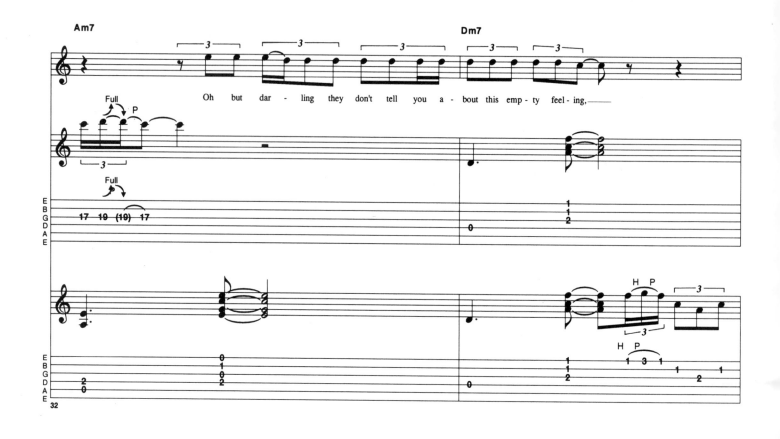

Oh but dar - ling they don't tell you a - bout this emp - ty feel - ing,

you know___ I can't dis - guise it.___

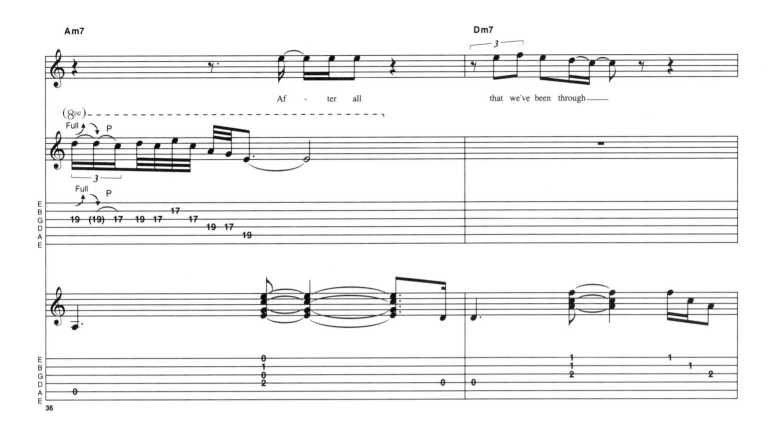

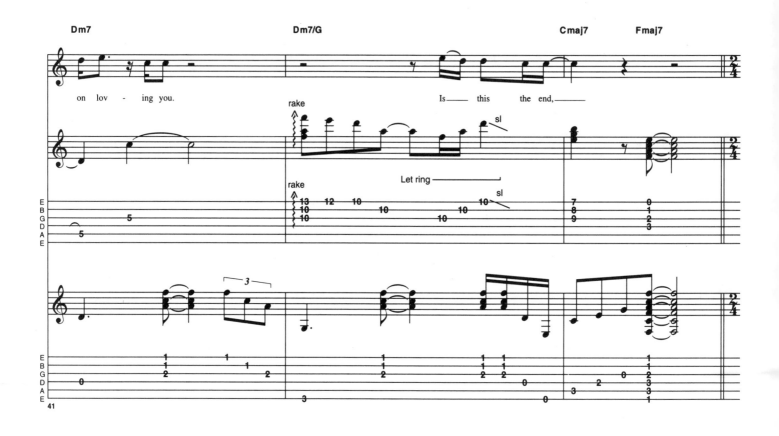

Dm7   Dm7/G   Cmaj7   Fmaj7

on lov - ing you.

Is —— this the end,

rake

Let ring

41

Am9   Am7   D/A

still in love—— with you.

Oh ——

With echo   With distortion

44

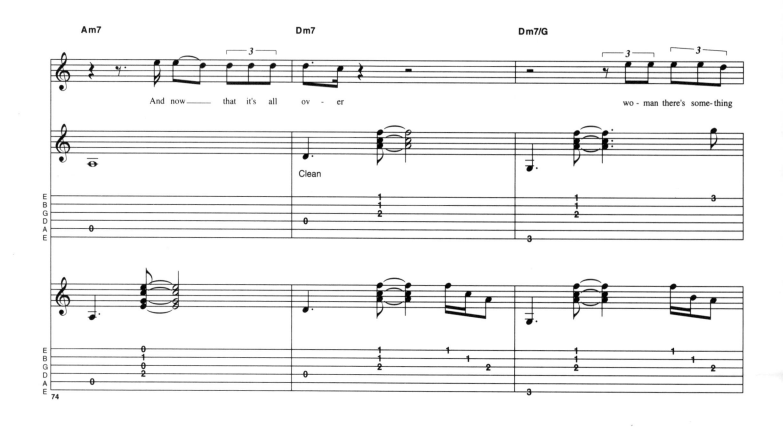

And now—— that it's all ov - er

Clean

wo - man there's some - thing

I think   you should know.——

Full

Full

Hey   may - be 'cause   my ba -

P

P

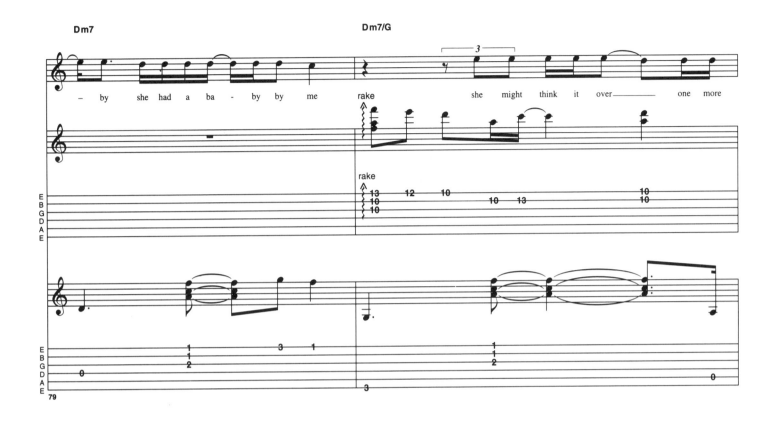

if there's an - y - thing I could do for you,

Full

call

rushed

on me ba - by,

rake

help me see it through.

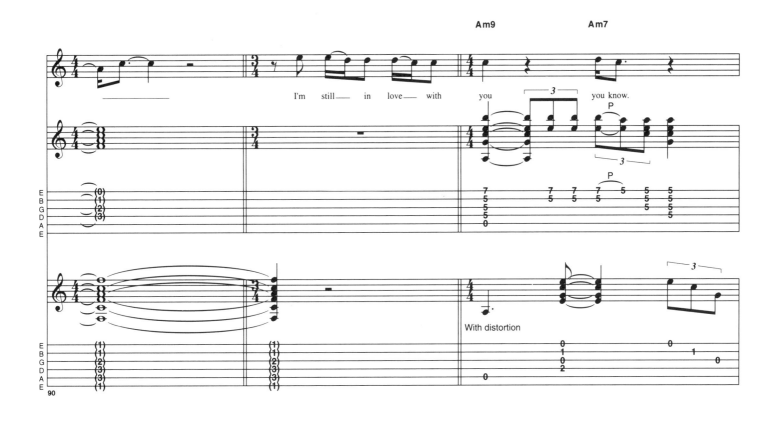

I'm still— in love— with you— you know.

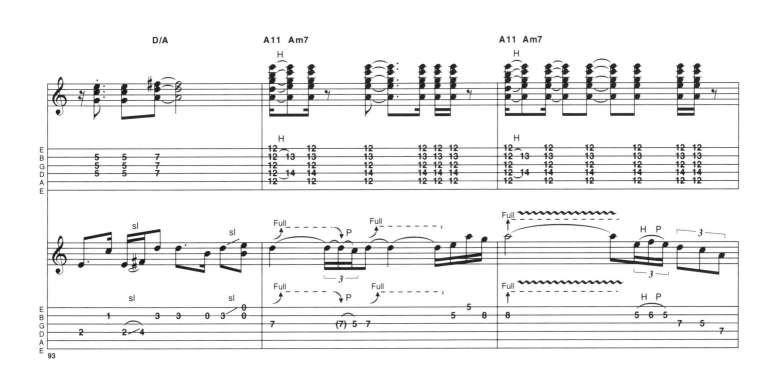

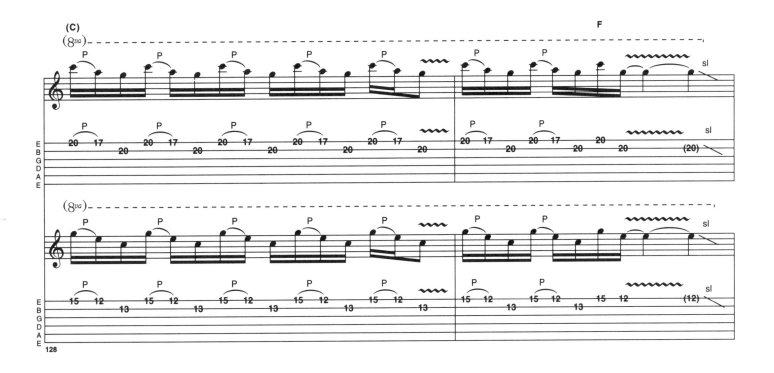

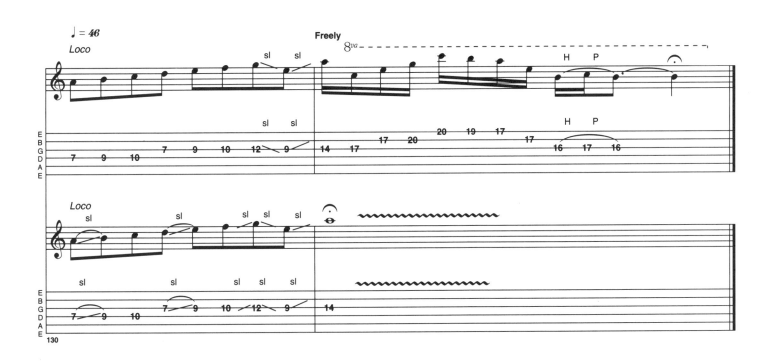

The Boys Are Back In Town

Words and Music by PHIL LYNOTT

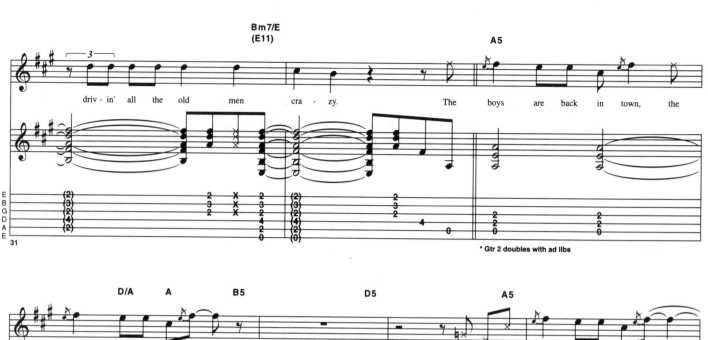

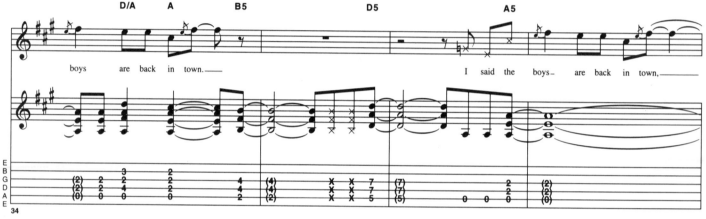

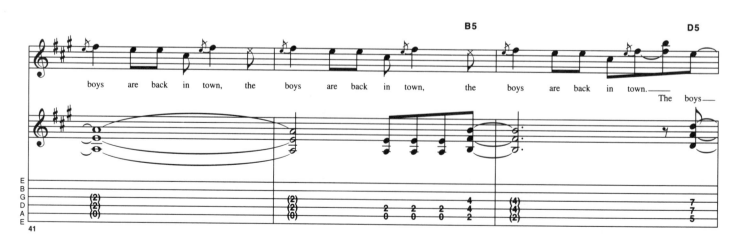

are back in town.

Gtr 1

Gtr 2

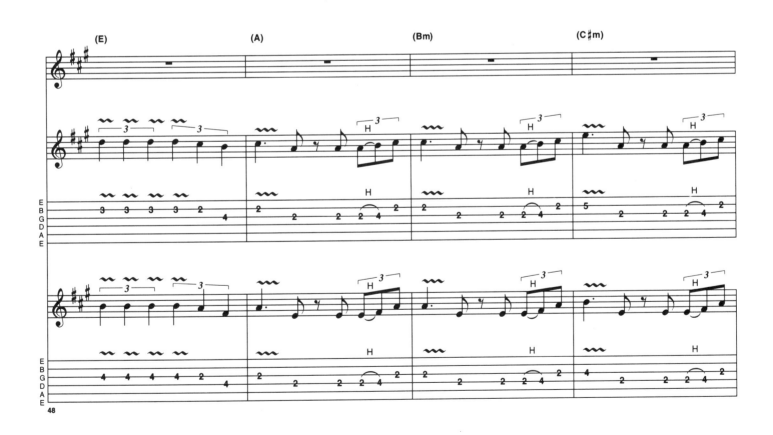

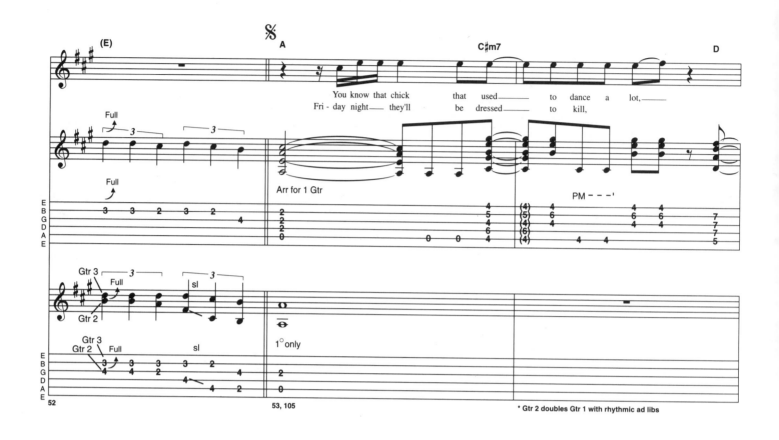

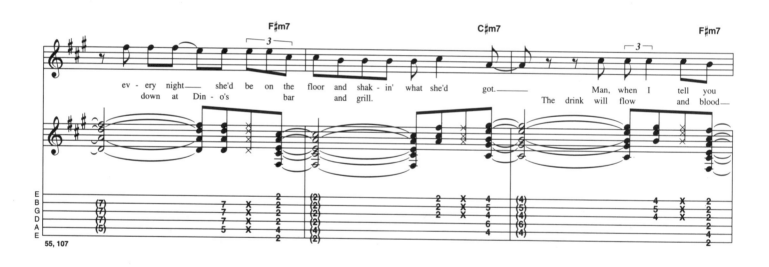

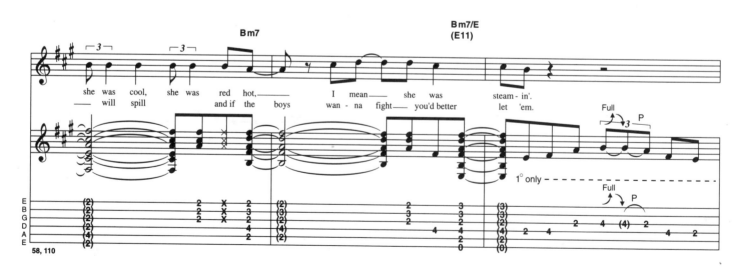

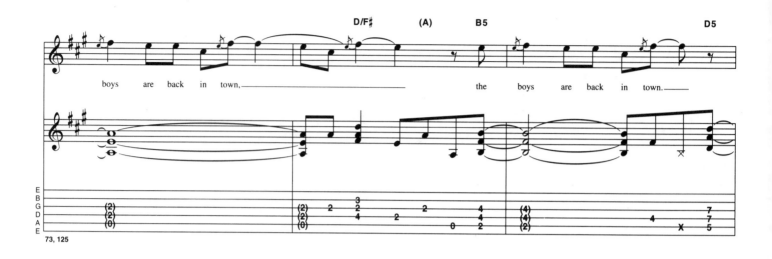

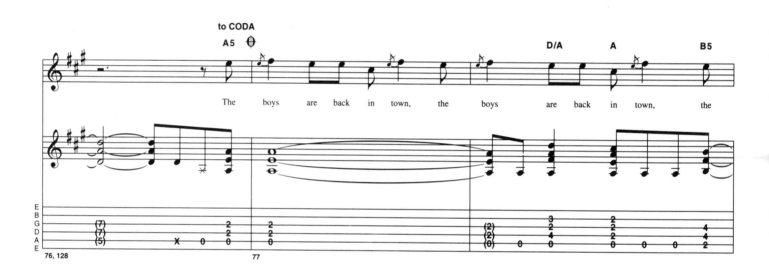

58

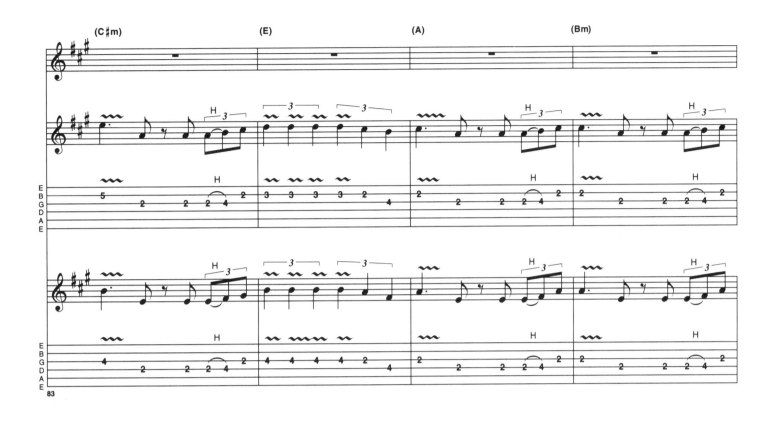

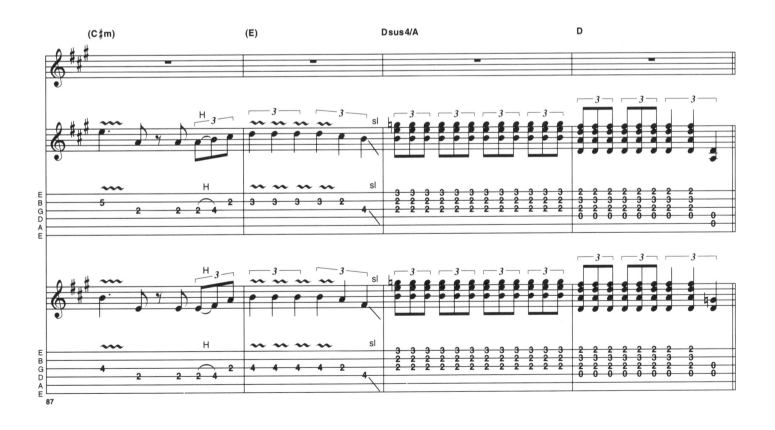

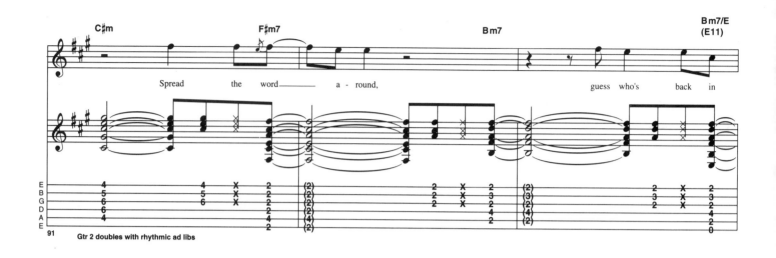

Spread the word a - round, guess who's back in

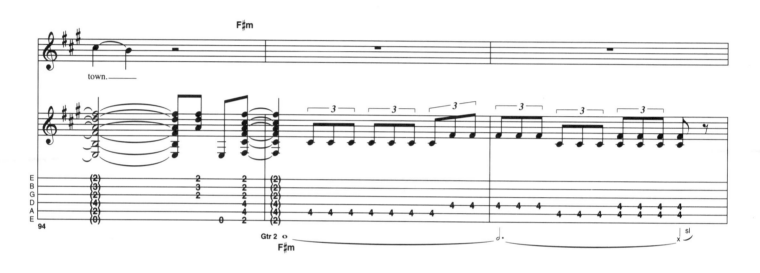

town.

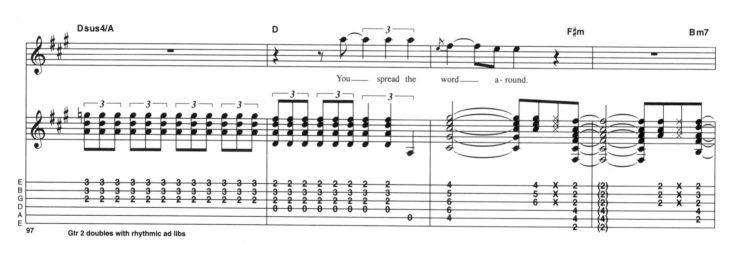

You spread the word a - round.

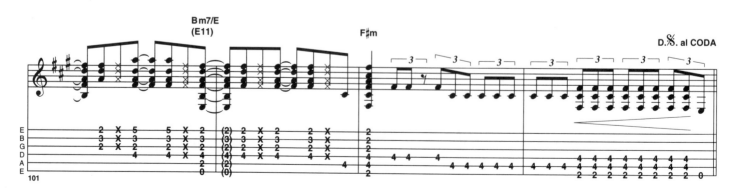

60

CODA

boys are back in town, the boys are back in town.— Spread the word a - round, the

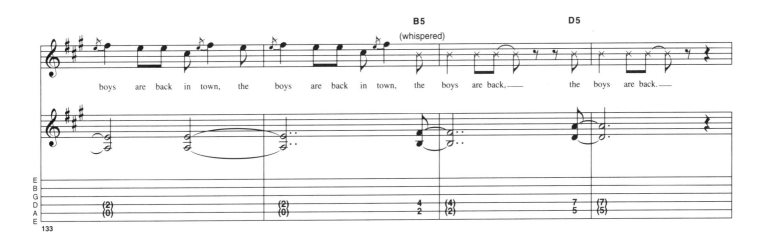

boys are back in town, the boys are back in town, the boys are back,— the boys are back.—

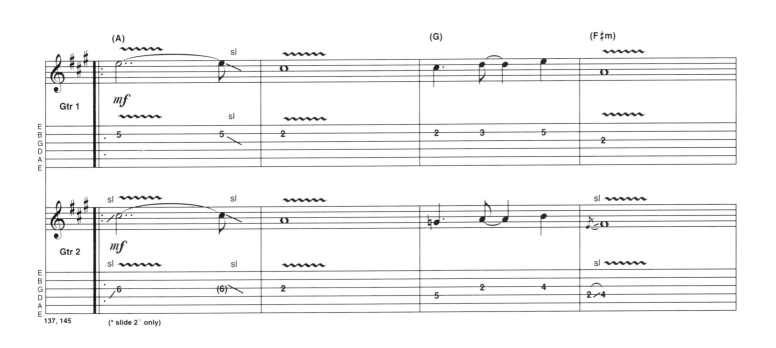

(* slide 2° only)

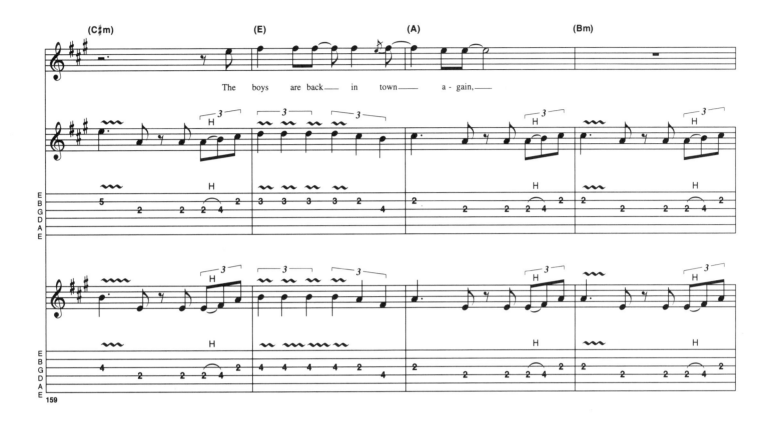

The boys are back___ in town___ a - gain,___

they're hang-ing___ down___ at Di - no's.___

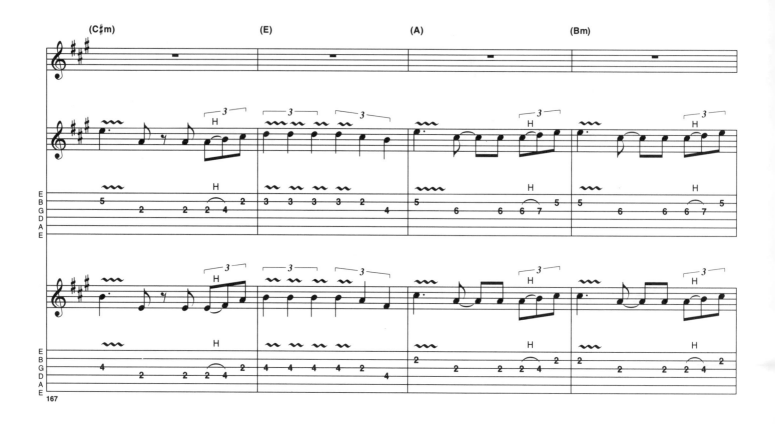

The boys are back— in town—— a - gain.——

Whiskey In The Jar

Arranged by ERIC BELL, BRIAN DOWNEY & PHIL LYNOTT

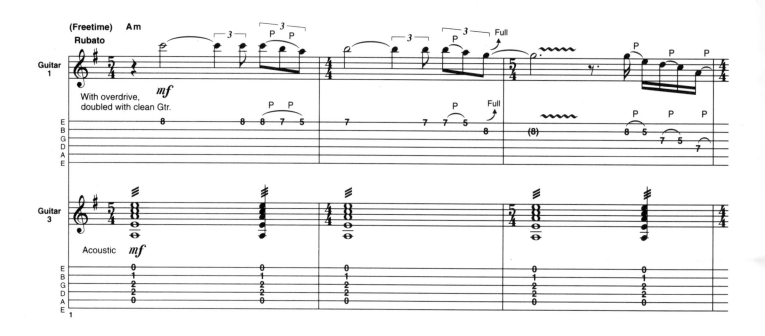

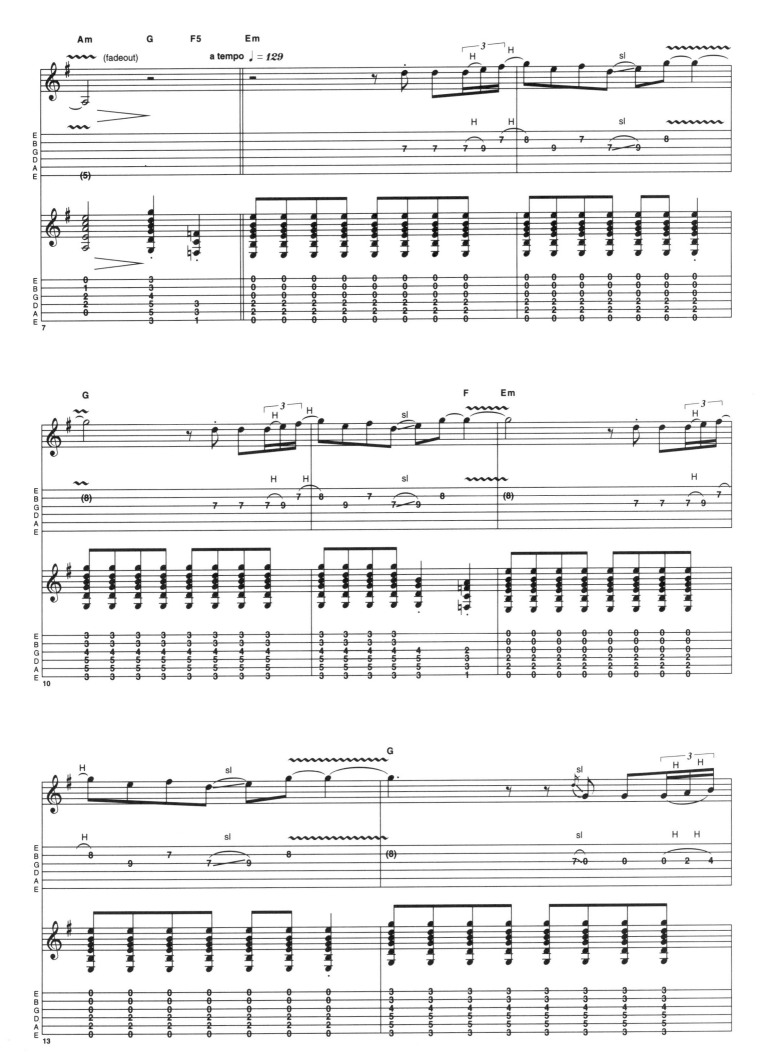

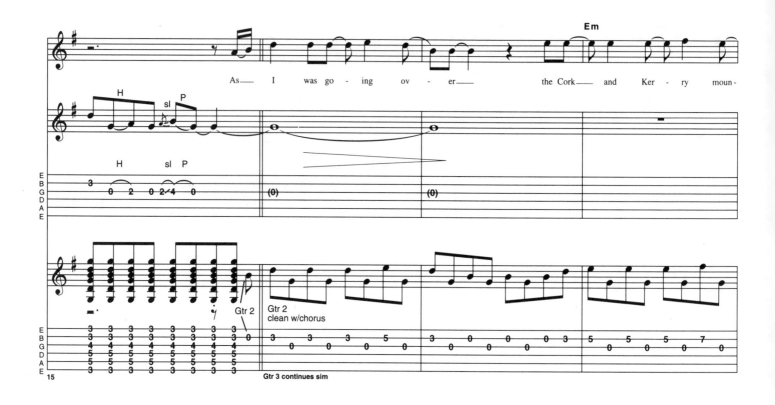

As— I was go - ing ov - - er— the Cork— and Ker - ry moun-

- tains— I saw Cap - tain Far - rell— and his mon-

- ey he— was coun - - ting. I first pro - duced— my pis -

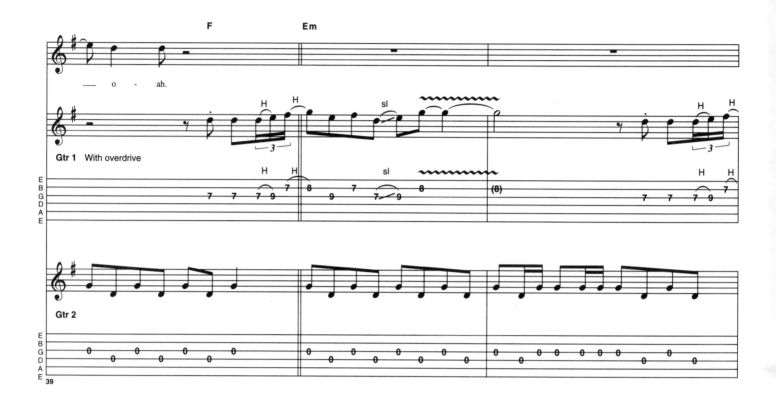

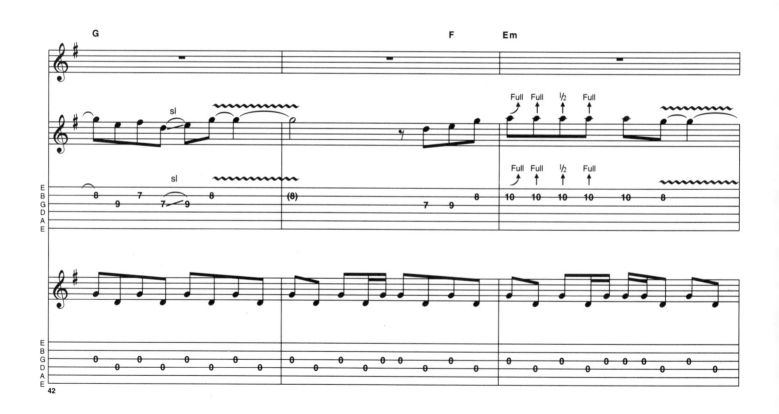

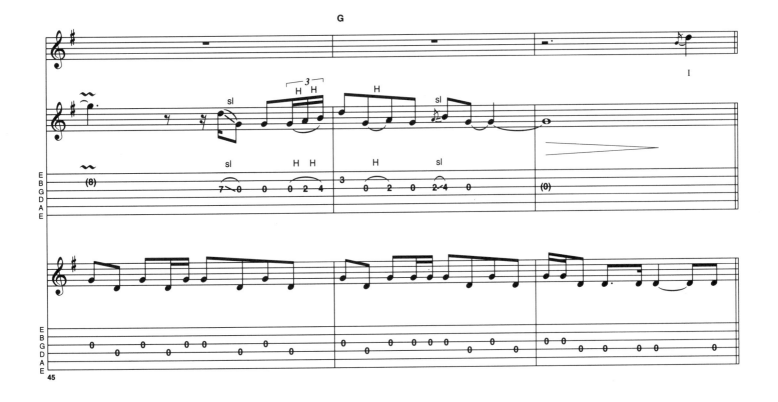

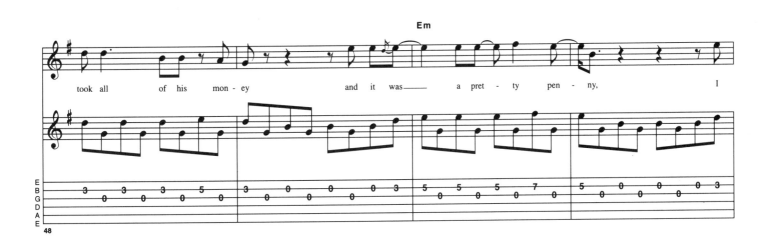

took all of his mon - ey and it was —— a pret - ty pen - ny, I

took all of —— his mon - ey and I brought —— it home —— to Mol - ly. She

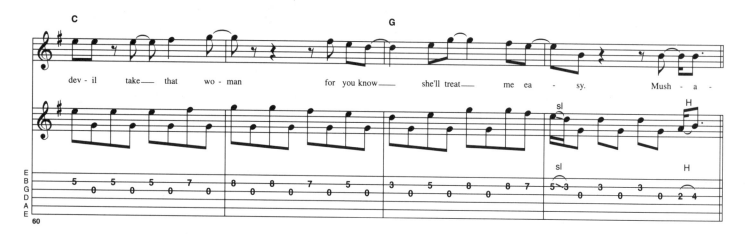

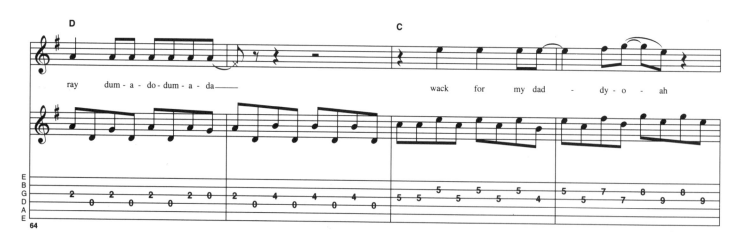

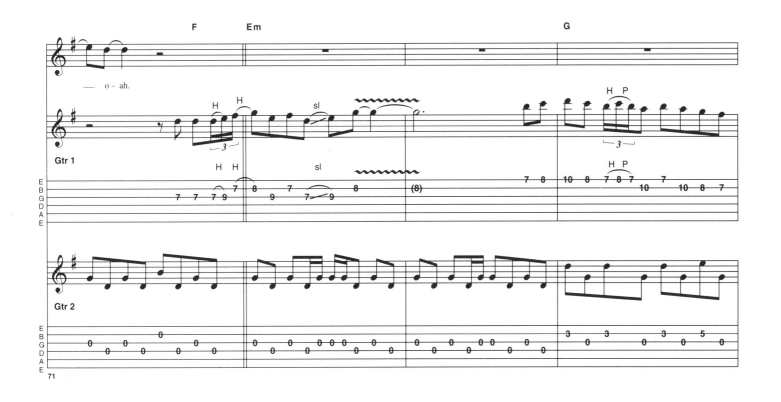

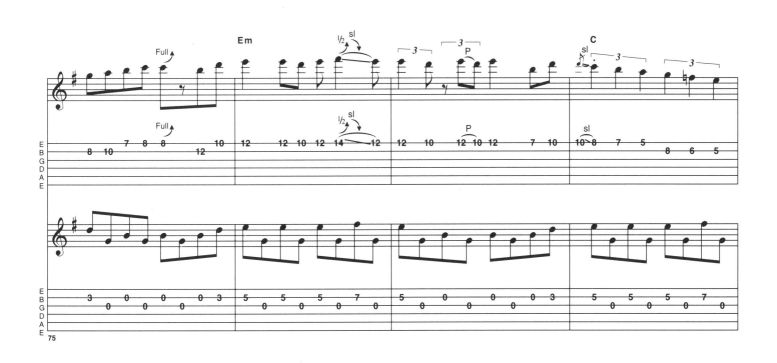

73

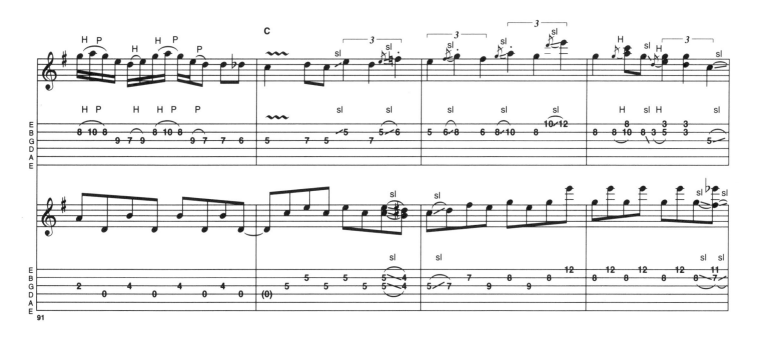

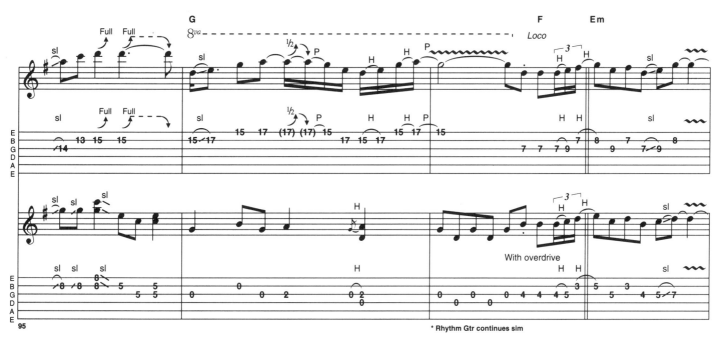

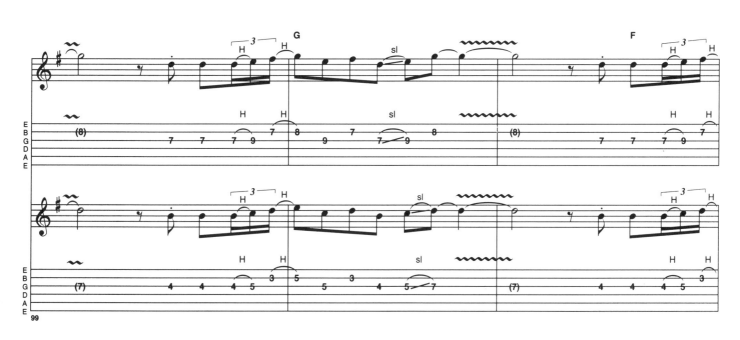

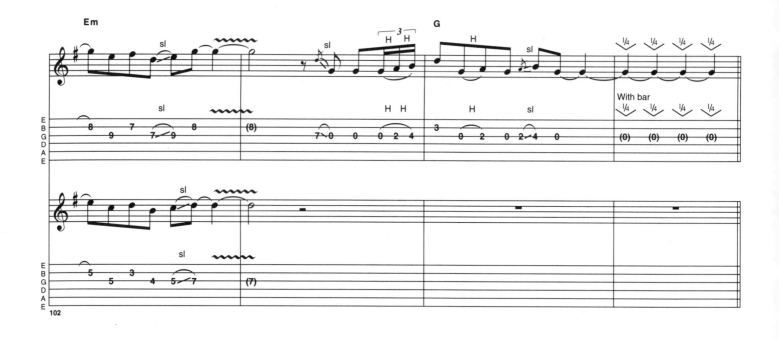

Being drunk and weary I went to Molly's chamber,

taking my money with me and I never knew the danger, for a-

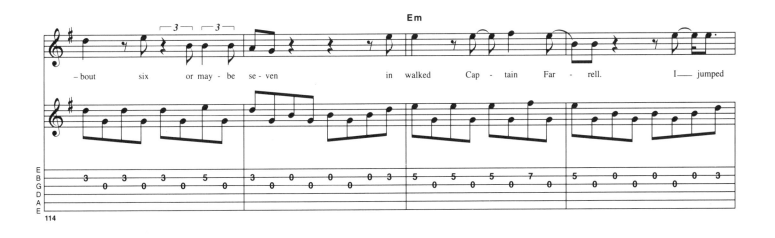

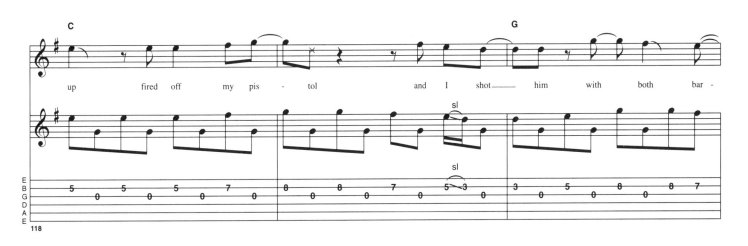

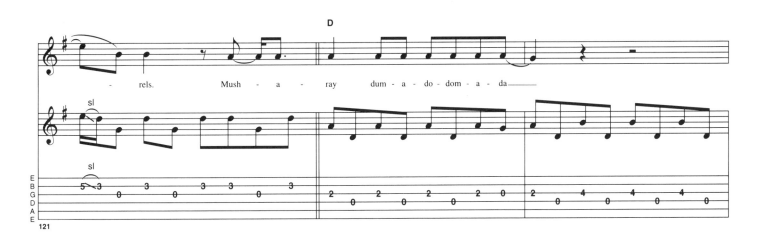

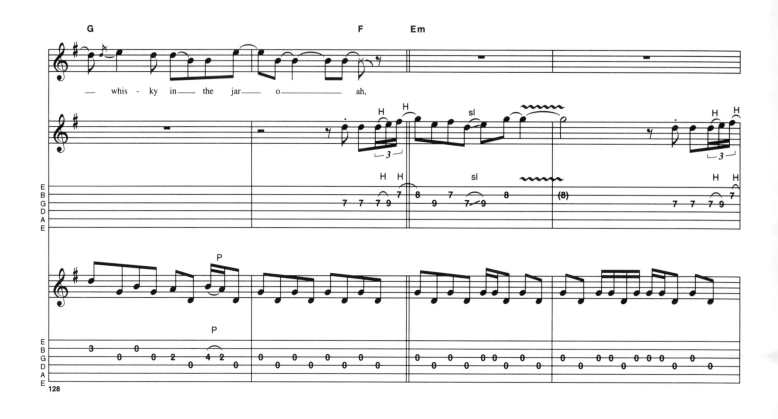

whis - ky in — the jar — o — — — ah,

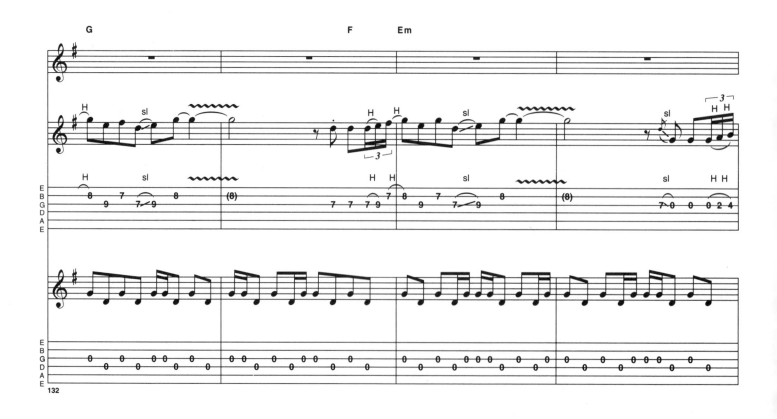

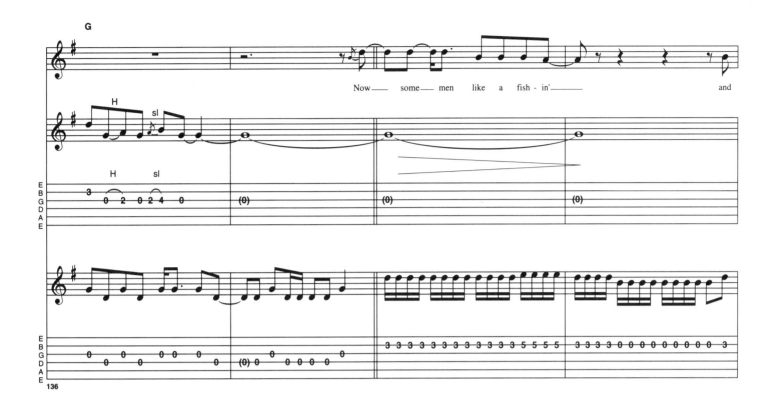

Now— some— men like a fish - in'——— and

some men like——— a - fow - - lin'——— and

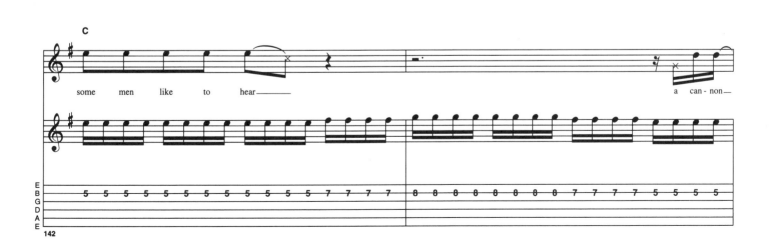

some men like to hear——— a can - non——

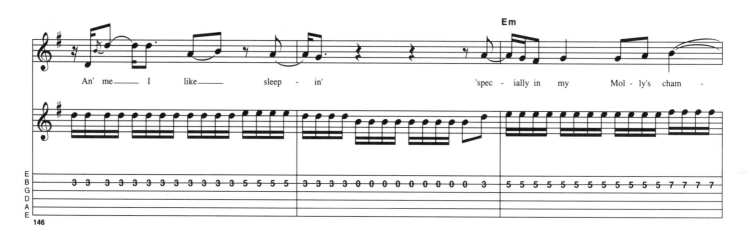

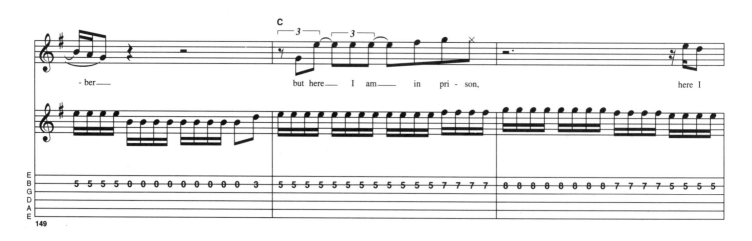

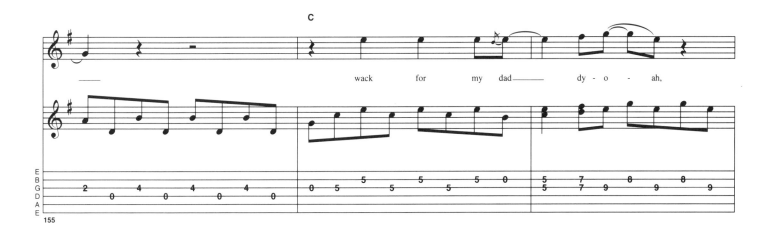

wack   for   my   dad_____ dy - o - ah,

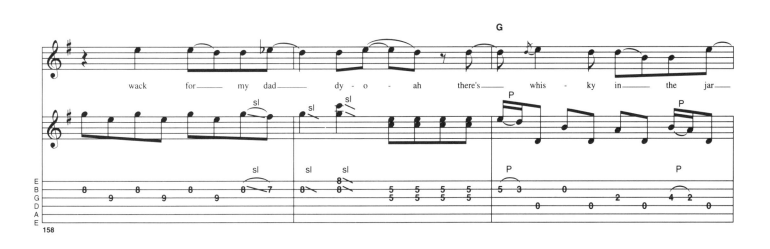

wack   for_____ my   dad_____ dy - o - ah   there's_____ whis - ky   in_____ the   jar_____

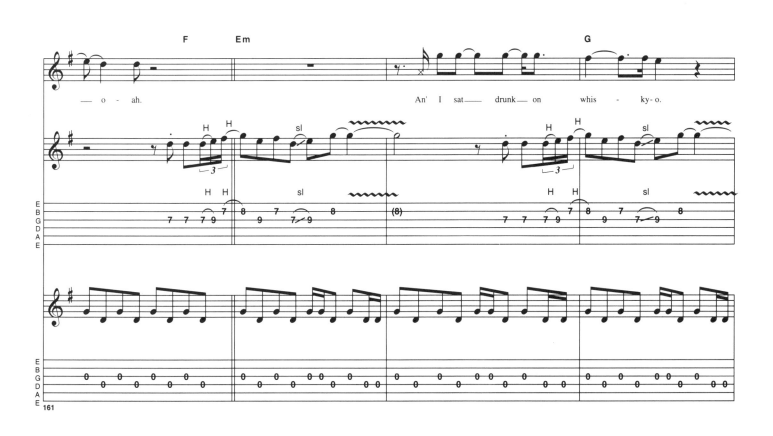

____ o - ah.   An' I sat_____ drunk_____ on   whis - ky - o.

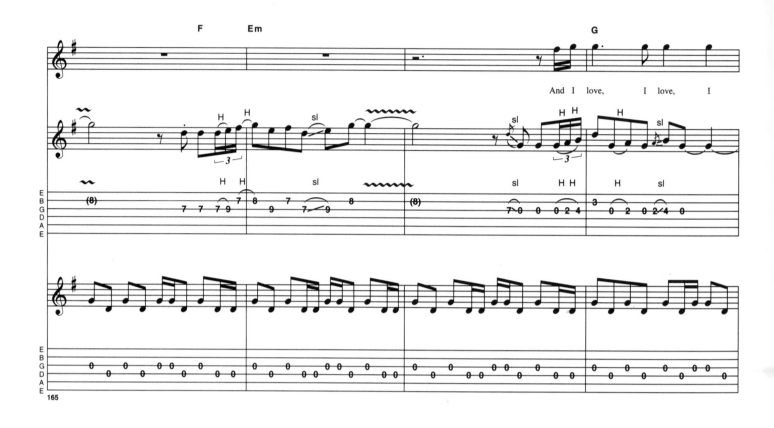

And I love, I love, I

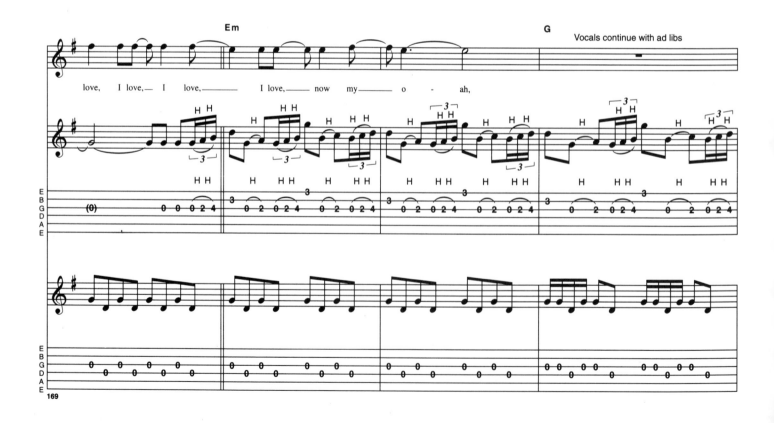

love, I love, I love, I love, now my o ah,

Vocals continue with ad libs

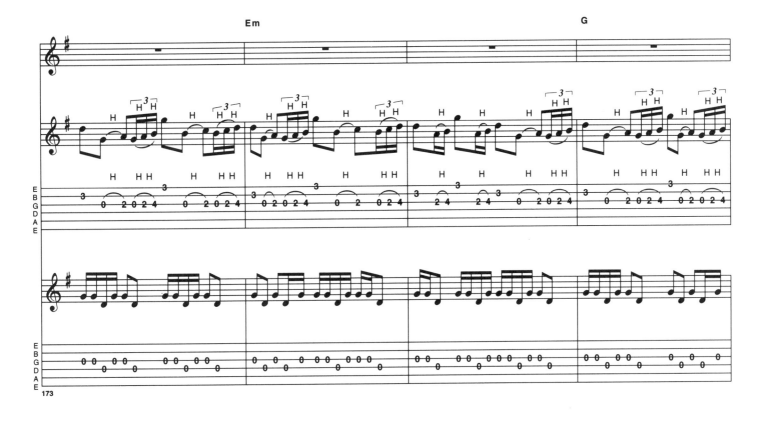

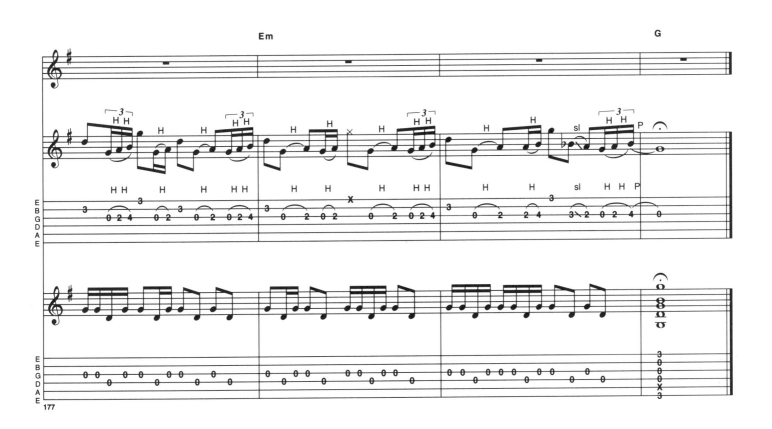

Jailbreak

Words and Music by PHIL LYNOTT

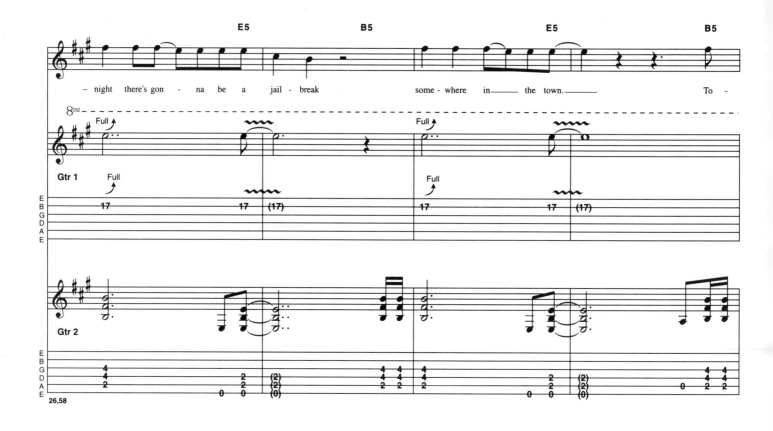

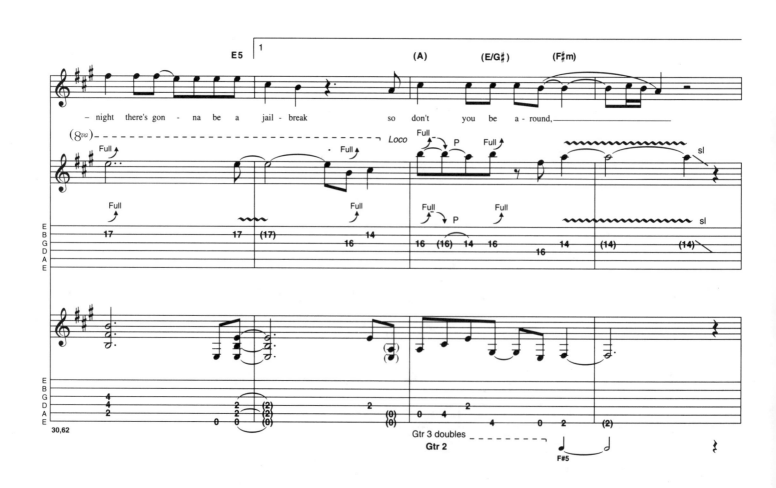

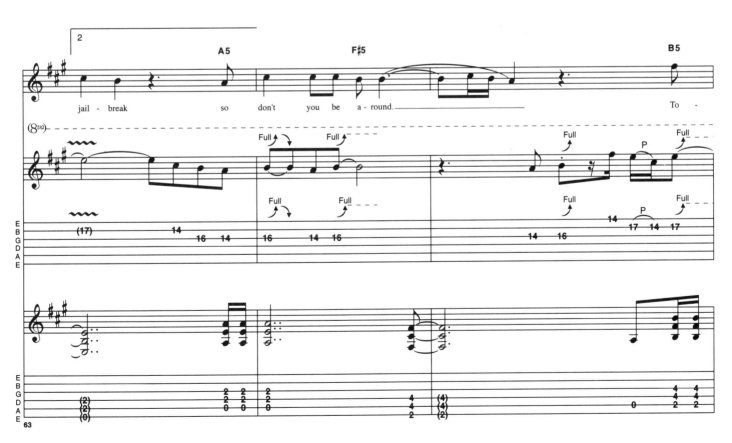

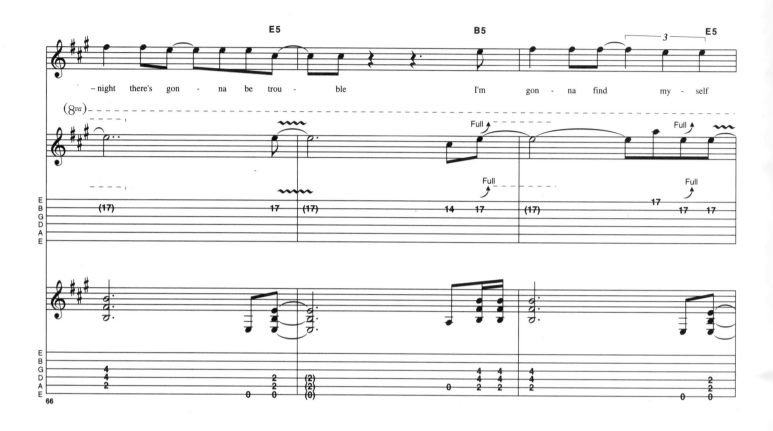

- night there's gon - na be trou - ble   I'm   gon - na find   my - self

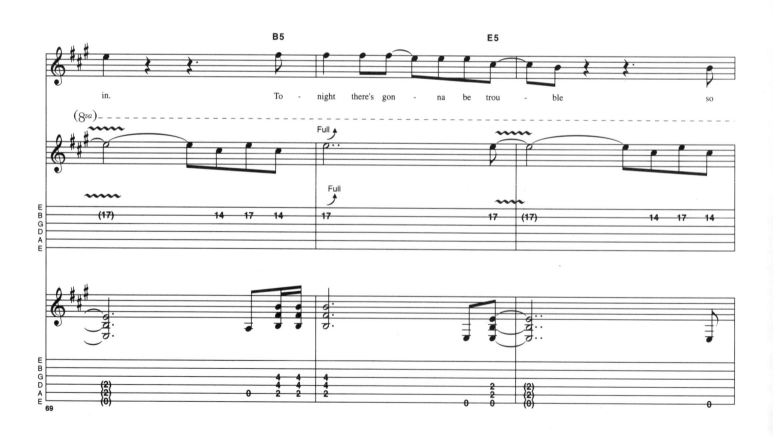

in.   To - night there's gon - na be trou - ble   so

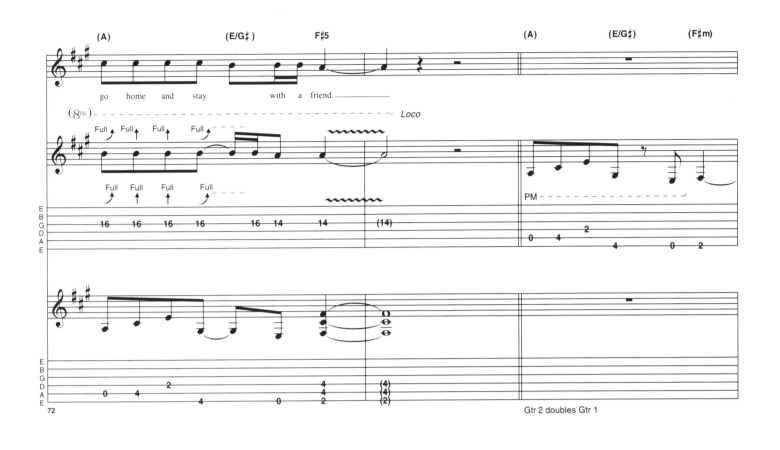

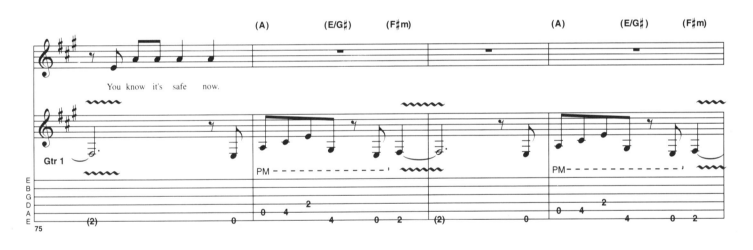

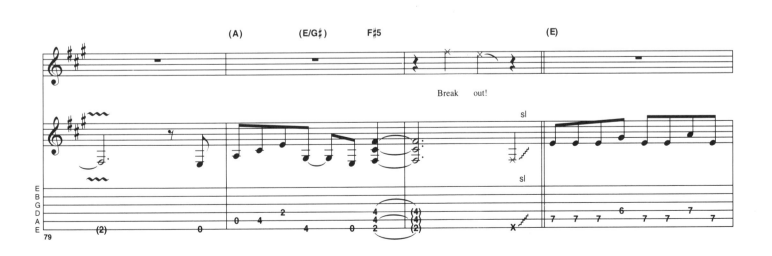

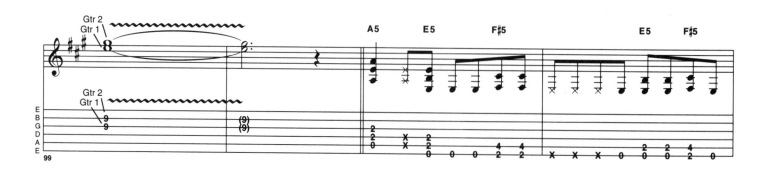

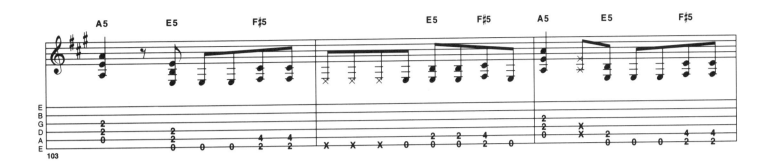

D. 𝄋. al CODA

To -

CODA

-night there's gon - na be a jail - break   some - where in —— this town.

91

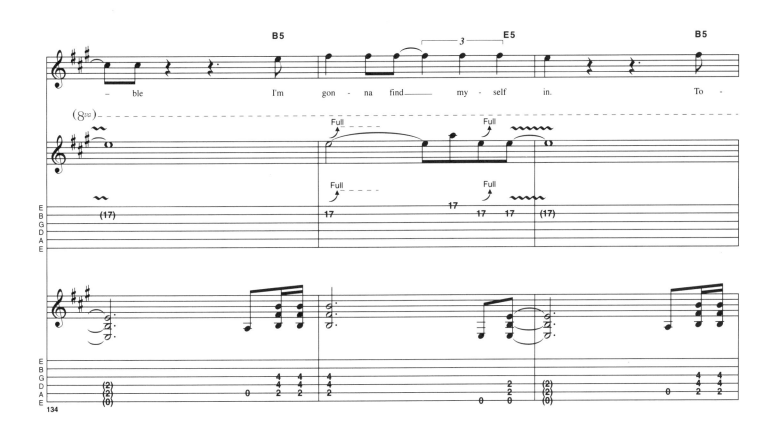

Rosalie

Words and Music by BOB SEGER

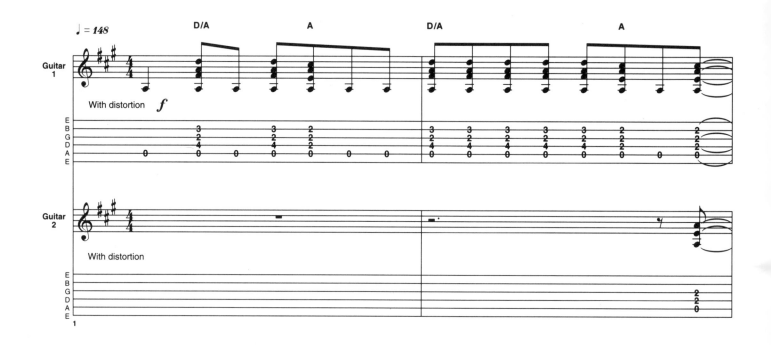

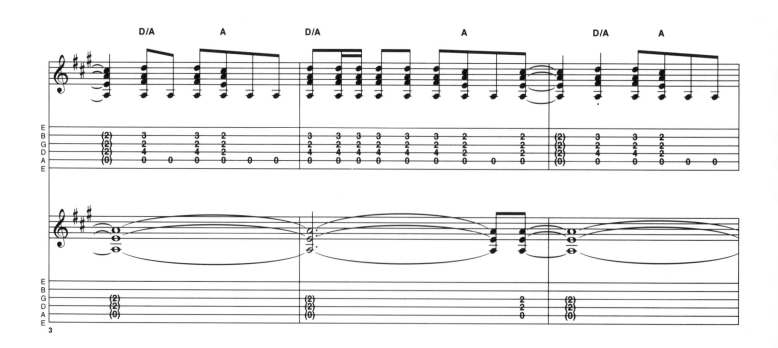

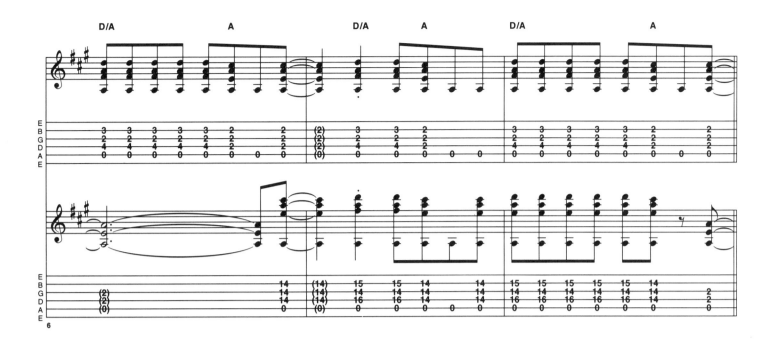

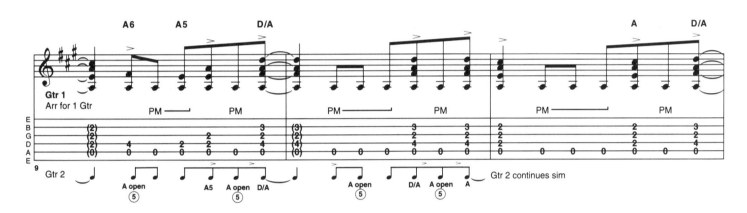

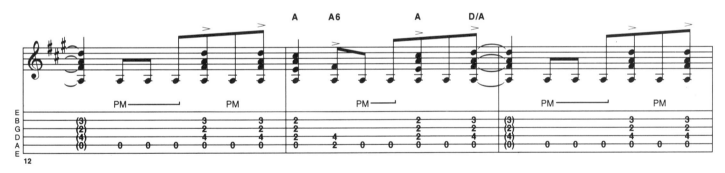

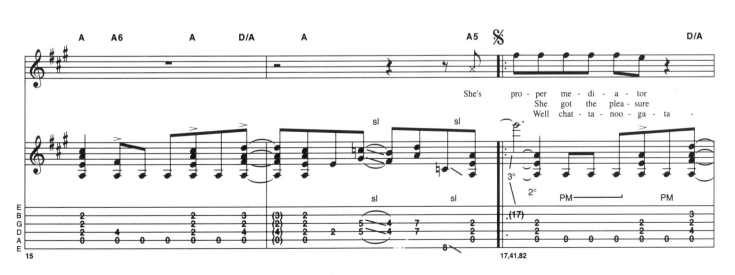

She's   pro - per   me - di - a - tor
She   got   the   plea - sure
Well chat - ta - noo - ga - ta -

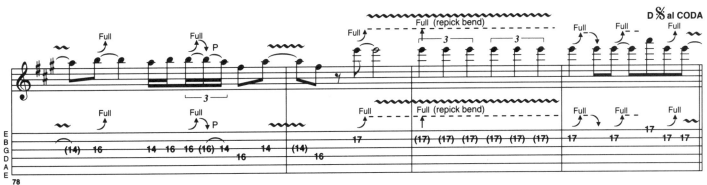

Hey you're clap-ping your hands   for me

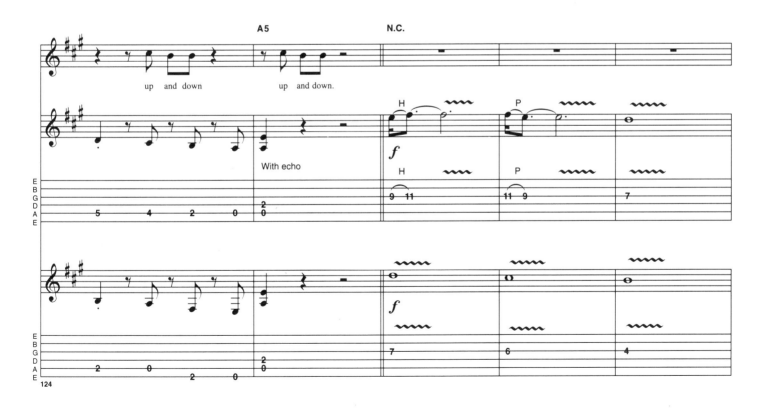

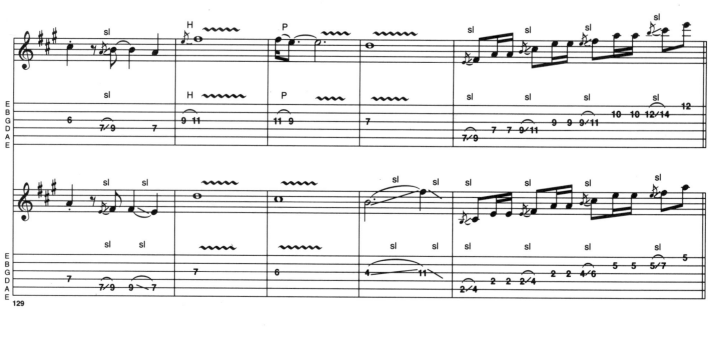

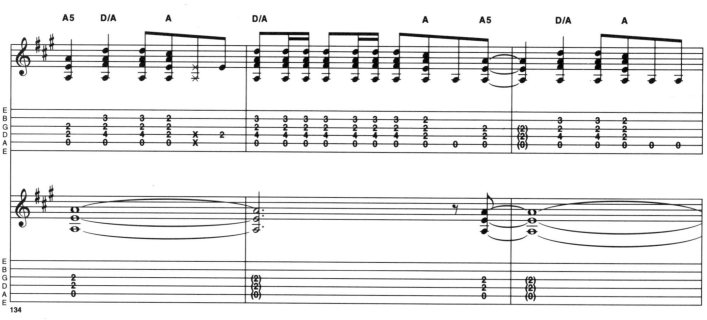

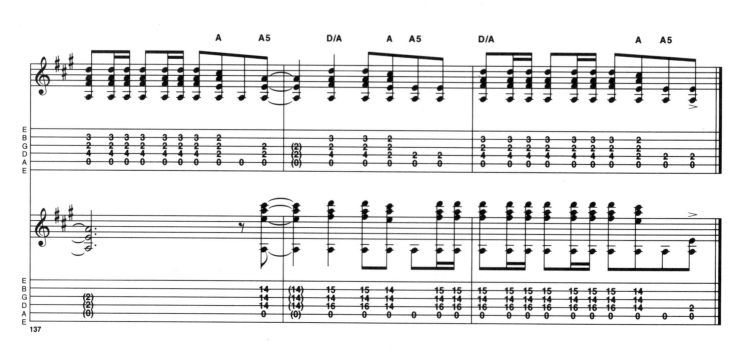

Emerald

Words & Music by PHIL LYNOTT, BRIAN DOWNEY,
SCOTT GORHAM & BRIAN ROBERTSON

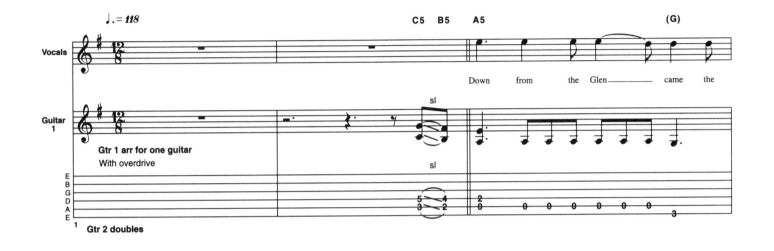

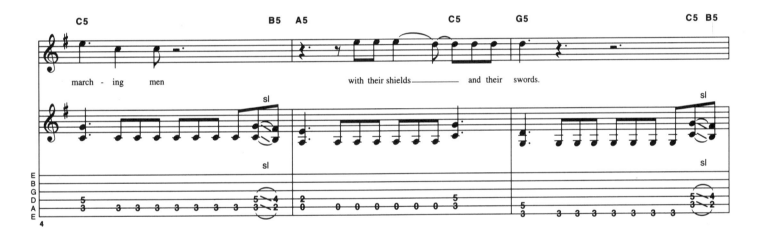

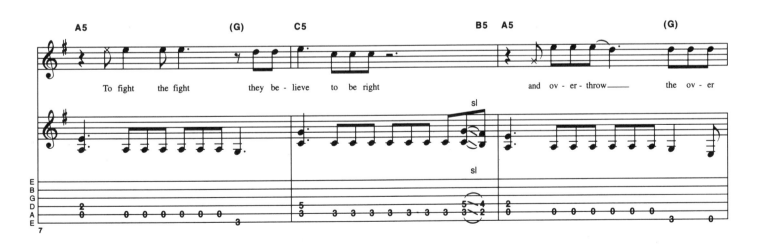

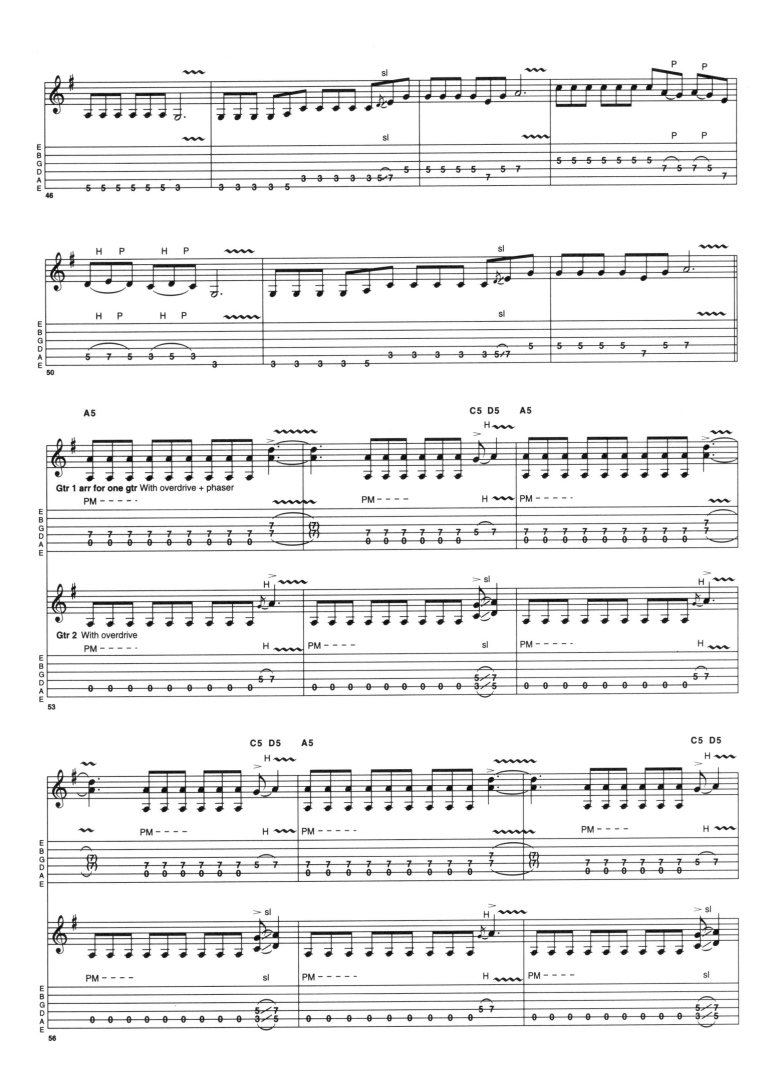

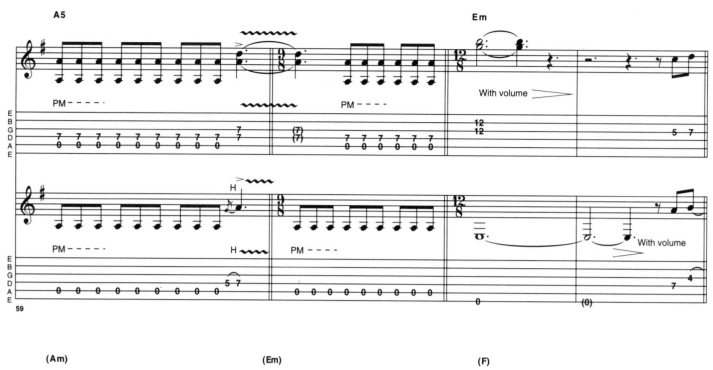

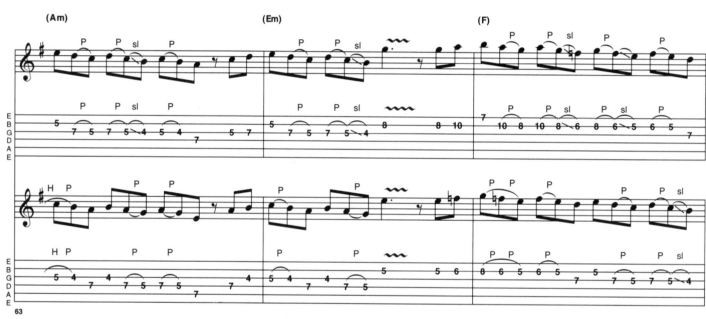

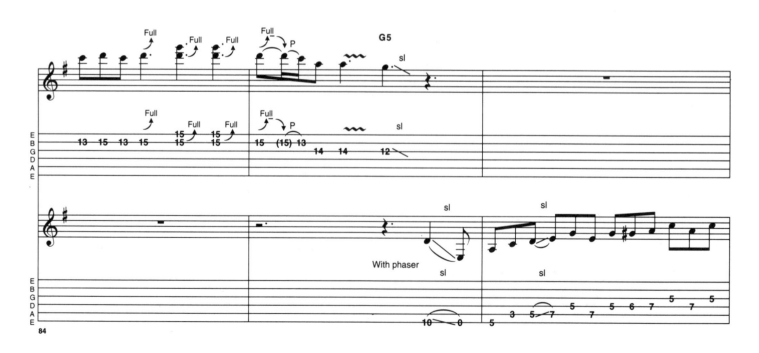

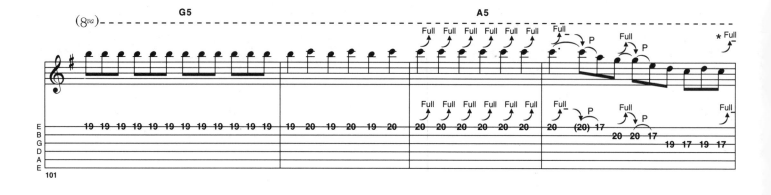

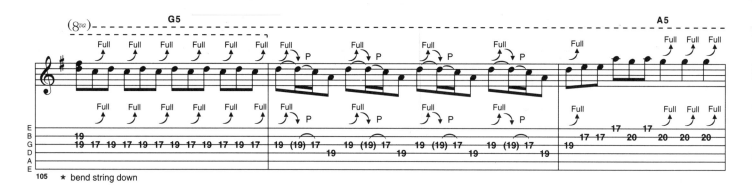

★ bend string down

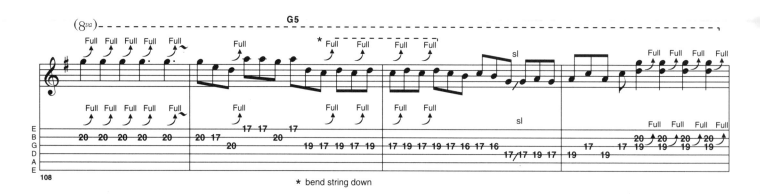

★ bend string down